THEN AND THERE SERIES
GENERAL EDITOR
MARJORIE REEVES, M.A., PH.D.

Cavaliers and Roundheads

ELEANOR MURPHY

Illustrated by

D. JARRETT and H. C. McBEATH

LONGMAN

THE LONDON ORATORY SCHOOL
Seagrave Road, S.W.6.   Telephone 01-385 0102

Department			Book Number		

Date of Issue	*	Name of Pupil	Form	Initials of Teacher
27/6/83	G	R. DUCCI	2CS	
25/6/86	G	Nigel Lynch	2FN	

*Condition: N – New; G – Good; F – Fair; P – Poor.

CONTENTS

TO THE READER

This is the story of the years when Charles I quarrelled with his Parliaments, and Cavaliers fought Roundheads because of it. We hope that reading this book will encourage you to find out about the Civil War in your own district.

You may find that you have a local hero, as Cornishmen had in Sir Bevill Grenville who fought for the King, or you may find, as at Pontefract, a story that is as exciting as any thriller. For example, I grew up in Newcastle upon Tyne. There you can learn about Sir John Marley, who persuaded the Town Council to support the King and who led the town during a bitter siege which lasted for eight months. You can also find out about the time when the King was a prisoner in Newcastle before the Scots handed him over to Parliament. Now I live in Sussex. There were many who supported the King in Sussex, but it was the Parliamentary supporters who were the more important people and they kept the county for Parliament. In Sussex, as in many districts, were friends who wrote to each other and remained friends even though they fought on opposite sides, and there were families which divided—one brother to support the King while another fought for Parliament. There were also farmers and country people who joined together to protect themselves against either side.

It is almost impossible to live anywhere in the British Isles and the Channel Islands without living in or near some place which tells an exciting story about the Civil War and which gives us some of the reasons why Cavaliers fought Roundheads.

About Spelling

In the seventeenth century, there was no fixed spelling. In printed books, words were written very much as we spell them today, but when people wrote to each other they usually spelled the words just as they sounded. It is quite easy to understand what was written if you read it aloud. In most cases where I have quoted from letters and diaries, the spelling has been modernised but I have left some passages as they were written just to let you see what they were like.

I

Civil War

On 22 August 1642, King Charles I raised his standard at Nottingham and called on his subjects to support him in his struggle with Parliament. On 9 September, an army marched out of London, on its way to fight for Parliament against the King. This was Civil War: war, not between two nations, but between two sides in the same nation. There was almost five years of it until the King was defeated in 1647. Then there was another short outbreak of civil war in 1648 when the King's forces were defeated again, and the King was executed in 1649. After that, there was eleven years without a King until Charles's son was restored in 1660.

Civil War is the worst of all kinds of war: it is a time when men have to take the terrible decision to fight against their own countrymen, sometimes against their own fathers and brothers and friends. People in 1642 had to choose between fighting for King or Parliament. For some men it was easy to decide which side they wished to support. For others it was a hard, sad decision which they had to make. Many did not want to support either King or Parliament and tried not to fight at all.

When we read the letters which men and women of that time wrote to each other, and the diaries they kept, we can see something of the heartache that many suffered

King Charles I

because of the Civil War. We can understand their sadness when a family split, some of them to support the King and some to fight for Parliament.

There are two families especially who tell us in their writings about life during the Civil War. One is the family of Sir Edmund Verney who lived at Claydon in Buckinghamshire. Sir Edmund had spent most of his life at

Court, and he supported the King. His eldest son was called Ralph. (In the letters of the Verney family, Ralph's name is often spelled 'Rafe', so that must have been how he pronounced it.) Ralph was a good son, devoted to his father and to his brothers and sisters. Despite the great love between his father and himself, however, Ralph stayed with Parliament though he knew his decision made his father very unhappy. In the end, Ralph found that he could not agree with Parliament, and so he had to go into exile in France because he could support neither King nor Parliament. The next son, Tom, was the black sheep of the family: everyone grew tired of trying to help Tom. He

Sir Edmund Verney

3

Ralph Verney

fought for the King with no great feelings about the war but simply for want of something to do. Then there was Edmund, named after his father and always known as Mun. He was a passionate supporter of the King and had no doubts at all about it: he simply could not understand Ralph. At first, the brothers quarrelled about it, but in the end, Mun apologized to Ralph and wrote: 'Howsoever your opinion and mine may differ in this, yet I beseech you remember that we are brethren still and love one another.' Henry, the youngest son, had always wanted to be a soldier. He is an example of one of the comparatively few men on either side who was a professional soldier and had learned to be one in wars abroad. He was,

4

however, really only interested in having a good time. He was in the King's army because that was where his friends were. Once the King had been executed, he was just as happy to go horse racing with his old enemies.

The Verneys were great letter writers, and hundreds of their letters to each other and to their friends have been preserved in their home at Claydon to this day. Many of these letters have been printed and so we can all read them. We can follow their lives during the war because they kept in touch with each other as much as they could. As you might expect, the letters were not all about politics or about the war. They still had clothes to buy, homes to look after and friends to meet. So thanks to the chance which has preserved their letters, we know a good deal about the way people lived then.

View of Claydon House today

Another family which illustrates the divisions caused by the Civil War is that of John Hutchinson and his wife, Lucy. Their home was at Owthorpe in Nottinghamshire. Until the war, they lived a quiet life in the country with

Colonel Hutchinson

their children, but John Hutchinson read a great deal about the disputes between the King and his Parliaments and, when war broke out, he decided to fight for Parliament. He became a colonel in the Parliamentary forces and held Nottingham for Parliament. The leader of the King's forces in the district was his favourite cousin, Sir John Byron. The two cousins fought bitterly against each other, partly because they both feared that others would say that they were not willing to fight against each other because of their friendship. Lucy Hutchinson's favourite brother, Allan Apsley, also fought for the King against Parliament. When the King's forces were defeated, John Hutchinson was therefore on the winning side and tried to help Allan. But when King Charles II came back to the throne in 1660, it was John Hutchinson who was in trouble because of his share in the execution of Charles I; then Allan tried to help his sister and brother-in-law. John Hutchinson died in prison, and his wife wrote the story of his life so that their children would know about their father and what he had fought for. She does not tell us so many interesting details of ordinary life as we can learn from the Verney letters, but she describes her husband so well that we can see that he was a good and honest man who be-

6

lieved that what he did in the war was the right thing to do.

That was the sad thing about the Civil War. There were many good and brave men on both sides. Although the Verneys and the Hutchinsons do not give us all the reasons why men joined in the quarrel between King and Parliament, yet we can learn much from them of why men became Cavaliers or Roundheads, and what it was like to live through those years of trouble in the Civil War.

2

The Verneys at Home

People do not always live in a new house which has just been built and which has all the contemporary ideas of what a smart house should look like and how it should be furnished. Some of us today live in very old houses, some of us live in houses built perhaps a hundred or fifty years ago, and only some of us live in brand new houses. It was just the same in the seventeenth century.

The home of Sir Edmund Verney and his children was over a hundred years old at the time of the Civil War. It was one of the brick Tudor houses which you must have learned about when you were studying the history of the sixteenth century in England. The central part of the house was narrow, and then there were wings on either side of it to make the house look like an E. There were no passages in the house, and you walked from one room to the other. The house still stands at Claydon today, but it has been altered a good deal. There is, however, a drawing of the house as it was in the seventeenth century and so we can see what it must have looked like then. Sir Edmund Verney's own room was the one above the porch.

If the Verneys had been building a new house about this time, it would probably have been rather different. The new houses of the day were square in shape, and the hall

Claydon House in the seventeenth century

ceased to be the most important room in the house. About the beginning of the seventeenth century, people stopped using the one big hall for everything, and had smaller rooms, each for its own particular use: the parlour, the dining-room and so on. You can see from the new houses which were built about this time that the hall is simply an entrance hall with the main living-rooms opening off it, which is all that our halls are today. The Verneys must have altered their old house a little so they could live like this, too, for they mention various rooms in their letters.

Most of the rooms of the time were panelled with wood, but people also covered the walls with leather or hung tapestries or embroidered linen from ceiling to floor. Rooms were often called by the colour of the hangings in the room: for example, there was an Orange room at Claydon. One of the Verney family's oldest friends, Lady

Sussex, had a set of tapestries which showed the four seasons of the year in one room, and she had a set of eight pieces with a design of flowers for another room. Carpets were just beginning to be used for the floors: Lady Sussex thought of buying one with a pattern of flowers on it. The Verneys had a carpet of leather in their dining-room, and this was usual in many homes.

A piece of seventeenth-century embroidery

Furniture changed a great deal in style in the early years of the seventeenth century. Although Sir Edmund Verney and Ralph lived in an old house, they evidently bought modern furniture for it: we can tell this from the furniture they mention in their letters. Perhaps one of the greatest changes in furniture at this time was that arm-chairs became popular. Up till then, there had been very few arm-chairs, and those were of wood. Only very important people had them, and everyone else sat on stools. Now, however, arm-chairs came into general use. Some were still made entirely of wood, but many had seats and backs of material. They had no springs, so they were still not as comfortable as ours are today, but the seats of satin or velvet, often stuffed, and with big cushions, must have made them much more comfortable than the wooden ones. One very popular style had X-shaped legs, with a covered seat and a back of fabric: here is an arm-chair in red velvet in which Charles I sat.

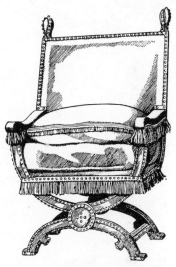

As well as arm-chairs, there were upright chairs and stools covered in material to match the arm-chairs, and studded with brass nails. The Verneys had a set of chairs and stools in crimson satin, and

Early seventeenth-century chair

another in red velvet. Lady Sussex had a set in crimson satin, and a set in blue velvet. Often the same material was used to cover chairs and to make hangings and curtains, so that everything in the room matched. Lady Sussex got Ralph to buy some satin so that she could furnish a room completely in one colour.

The dining-room had a long table, with a draw leaf at each end so that it could be made bigger when necessary.

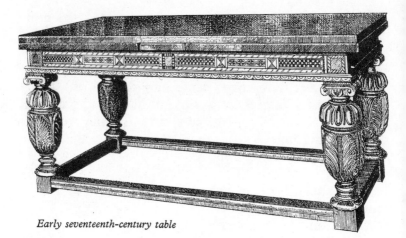

Early seventeenth-century table

On the table they used silver and *pewter* dishes. There were also wooden plates called trenchers, but these were mainly for the children and the servants. At night there were silver candlesticks on the table. Most people had

A wooden armchair

plain wooden chairs for their dining tables, like the one in the drawing, but the Verneys must have had chairs with seats and backs of material in their dining-room as well as in their parlour, for when Mary Verney went to Claydon to see what the house looked like after their absence in France, she wrote to Ralph to say that their dining-room chairs were in rags. The other pieces of furniture which you would be likely to see in a dining-room of this time were a court cupboard

Court cupboard

on which the silver and pewter dishes could be shown when they were not being used, and a buffet from which the food was served.

The most important piece of furniture in each bedroom was the great fourposter bed. The beds had a frill or vallance round the top, heavy curtains which were drawn round the bed at night (for people thought that fresh air was harmful) and an elaborate bedspread, all to match. Curtains and bedcovers were made of velvet, chinz or of embroidered materials. Lady Sussex had a bed with all its hangings in red satin, while the bedspread and vallance had a gold and silver fringe. She liked some linen hangings spotted with gold which she saw in a friend's house, and asked Ralph to look out for a set like that when he was in London. The sheets were often embroidered, too: Lady Sussex had some with a border at the top of gold and lace. The hangings were very expensive to buy. When Ralph decided that he needed two more curtains and a new valance for one of the beds in his house, they cost him almost £30. That means they would cost almost £300 nowadays— and yet that was not for the complete set of hangings needed for a bed then.

Apart from the bed, however, there was little else in the bedroom except, perhaps, some chairs and stools. There were no wardrobes then, and clothes were hung in small rooms which opened off the bedroom. These were known as fripperies. If you go to a newly built school and have a book-room opening off your classroom, then you will know exactly what Lady Verney's frippery, in which

A seventeenth-century bedroom at Knole House, Kent

14

she hung her dresses, was like. If there was no frippery, clothes had to be kept in chests.

When a husband or wife died, the widow or widower changed all the hangings in the bedroom to black ones. Just as they wore completely black clothes themselves, so people put their bedrooms into mourning. They had black curtains, black bedhangings, even black sheets. The Verneys had a mourning set of thirteen pieces, including black hangings for the walls. This was borrowed by all their friends and neighbours in Buckinghamshire when there was a death in the family: on one occasion, the set of mourning hangings was sent up to Yorkshire to relations there. When you realize how much some of the hangings for the bed alone cost Ralph, it is no wonder that friends borrowed the 'mourning bed' from each other, meaning by that, not the bed itself, but all the hangings and covers.

A country house at this time was completely self-supporting. Everything needed by the household was made on the premises. It was not just that they baked their own bread, prepared and preserved all their food, but they made almost all the goods needed in the house. At Claydon, there was a preserving-room where all the jams and jellies were made. There was a still-room where they made syrups, like the one made of violet petals, and vinegars such as raspberry vinegar. Sugar was only just beginning to come into England about this time, and foods and puddings were usually sweetened with honey or with syrups made from their own fruits and flowers. They also made their own wines, for there was no tea, coffee or chocolate to drink: it was just before 1660 when these began to come into the country as luxury drinks. Instead, people drank ale which they brewed at home, or the home-made wines made, again, from their own flowers and fruits.

15

A seventeenth-century farmyard

Outside the house, there was a dairy where the butter was made, a slaughter-house where their own animals were killed to give them meat, a spicery where the meat was preserved for the winter. There was a sawmill for any timber needed in the house or farms, and for cutting up firewood. Claydon also had its own blacksmith who shoed the horses, made and repaired bolts and locks, and made Sir Edmund Verney's helmet for him and repaired his armour. There were fishponds so that they could have fresh fish to eat, dovecots so that they could have pigeons as a change from the salt meat which they had to eat in the winter, and deer in the park to give them venison. Both Sir Edmund and Ralph were generous to friends who lived in London, and so could not get this fresh food. Presents of fish pies and pigeon pies were often sent to friends: one pie had forty-one pigeons in it! They often sent venison, too, as a present. When they themselves had to stay in London food was sent up from Claydon to their town house.

About this time, men began to take an enormous pride in their gardens. When Ralph Verney came back to Claydon from France in 1653 but was not allowed to take his seat in Parliament or to take any part in public affairs, he kept himself busy by planning and making a garden. He planted tulips (a new flower introduced from Holland) wallflowers and pinks. He paid a great deal of attention to the fruit trees in his garden: pear trees, cherry trees, walnut and apple trees were among those he planted. He also had vines and figs. Here is a garden from about the

A formal garden

time Ralph was planting his: the garden at Claydon must have looked very much like this when he had finished. You will see the complicated pattern of the flower-beds in the middle. It was very fashionable to make flower-beds like these: they were called knots. The pattern was marked out with box or low shrubs like lavender, and then the beds were filled in with flowers. This was probably why Ralph bought the pinks and wallflowers.

In the kitchen garden, Ralph Verney grew lettuce, cauliflowers, cabbages and asparagus. He had the plants sent over from France when he came back, but his uncle did not think that they were any better than the plants he could have got in England. Salads were eaten a great deal, and flowers like rosemary, violets, broom and cowslips were used in them. We do not know whether Ralph planted potatoes in his garden, but they were a new vegetable which people were only just beginning to plant and to eat about this time.

All this, of course, could only be done in a house in the country like Claydon. The Verneys had a house in London, too. Sir Edmund bought one because he had to be there so often when he was at the Court, and it gave him, and later Ralph, a home of their own to live in when they were in London to attend Parliament, or when they were doing their business. Their house in Claydon was an old one, but they lived in the very newest of houses in London for Sir Edmund bought one that had just been built at Covent Garden in 1634.

London and Westminster were then two separate towns, with only a straggle of big houses between them. In the 1630s, the Earl of Bedford laid out the old Convent Garden of Westminster Abbey with new houses, a church, a covered walk called a Piazza, all designed by the great architect of the day, Inigo Jones. It became very fashionable to live in these new houses at Covent Garden (as the name became). Many M.P.s had a house there because it was so convenient for Parliament. Denzil Hollis, who was one of the five members whom Charles I tried to arrest, lived there quite near to the Verneys. Later, Ralph moved to a new brick house not far away in Lincoln's Inn Fields.

These new houses were quite different from the old timber houses with overhanging storeys, and they set the pattern for all the new houses for many years in the future, though they did not become general until Londoners had to rebuild their houses after the Great Fire of London in 1666.

When the Verneys were travelling backwards and forwards between the two houses, they usually travelled on horseback. They had a coach drawn by four horses, but it was so uncomfortable that they preferred to ride. Coaches then had no springs in them, nor had they any windows. If it was cold and wet, there were leather curtains to draw across to try to keep the wind and rain out. The roads were so bad that the coach often got stuck in the mud. The Verneys' coach was often caught in the mud and the ruts round Aylesbury, and cart-horses had to be sent to pull it out. Like the house, the coach and horses were draped in black if anyone in the family died. When Sir Edmund Verney's wife died, he ordered that the saddles of the horses should be covered in black cloth and that the horses' bridles were to be black.

Coach with two horses

19

Riding pillion (a German, not an English, picture)

Ladies rode on their horses, too, rather than in a coach, if they could manage it. They usually sat side-saddle behind a servant: riding pillion, they called it. When one of Mary and Ralph Verney's babies was sent away from the smells of London to live in the fresh country air at Claydon, the baby was carried in a basket with cushions in it, strapped to the horse, while his nurse rode pillion on another horse beside him. It was too far for her to carry the baby in her arms all that way and yet travelling on horseback with the baby in a basket was more comfortable than being in the coach.

There were regular services of carriers who sent long wagons once or twice a week from towns all over the country to London. These carried both goods and passengers. Lady Sussex often wrote from her home in St Albans to ask the Verneys to shop for her in London. When Ralph was able to buy the things she asked for, he sent them by the regular carrier from London to St Albans, where she arranged for one of her servants to collect them from the yard and bring them to her home. The food and extra furnishings which the Verneys wanted in their London home when they were staying there, were sent by the carrier's wagon which went between London and Aylesbury, and then they sent a servant to collect it.

The Verneys, and indeed most people of the time, seem to have preferred to send the letters they wrote to each other by the carriers, or by a friend who happened to be going in the right direction, rather than trust the new postal system. From 1635, letters could be sent by a regular service of postmen who left London each day for the main towns. It cost 2d for 80 miles, 4d from 80 to 140 miles, and 6d above that. At the large towns, the local postmaster collected the postbags from the postmen travelling along the main roads, and then he sent the letters out by other men who would go to the neighbouring towns and villages to blow a horn to announce that they had arrived with the letters. One disadvantage of the postal system then was that unless the town you were writing to was on the same main road as the town you were writing from, the letters had to be taken up to London to be sent out again on the correct post road. There was no way of sending a letter across country by post. This added to the expense because of the extra miles it took for the letter to go up to London and out again.

The Verneys lived in troubled times. Even before civil war broke out, people were suspected of plotting against the government and so their letters in the post were opened. Sir Edmund Verney, writing to Ralph, said in one letter: 'I fear many of my letters are not come into your hands, or, if they have, yet I believe they have been opened . . . for now we have gotten that curiosity here to examine who sends news to London. Because I am confident of this bearer, I will tell you truly how I conceive things go here.' After war started, the post system often broke down. Although the King was executed on 30 January 1649, it was 21 February before Ralph's uncle could write to him because all the post was stopped to prevent people writing to each other about the King's death. When Oliver Cromwell was in power, his postmaster, John Thurloe, was able to keep Cromwell informed of plots against him by opening letters.

So most people preferred to send their letters by the carriers or to trust them to friends. There were no envelopes then, so people folded the sheet of paper on which they had written their letter, leaving one side free for the address. There were no numbers to the houses or fixed addresses as we have now, and so it was necessary to write a description of where the house was to be found. This is useful to us now, for the address on the letter often tells us something about the house. Here is the address on a letter to Ralph Verney when he was living at his new house in London: 'for Sir Rafe Verney att his hose in Lincolns Inn fields in the middle of the row were the Spanish Embassidor lies'. The address of one of Ralph's friends was 'A great house in Chancery Lane, over against Loncoln's Inne, near the Three Cranes, next dor the Hole in the Wall, within two dors of Mr Farmer's and one dor of Judge Ackings'.

3

The Clothes They Wore

There are many portraits to show us what men and women wore in these years before and during the Civil War. Some of their clothes have survived, too, and you can still see them in museums.

It was a time of great change in fashion. Men no longer wore the stiff padded breeches which had been fashionable in the days of Queen Elizabeth and James I, while *farthingales* and the stiff hooped skirts went completely out of fashion for women. Neither men nor women wore ruffs any more. The favourite materials for clothes, the hair styles—everything changed quite quickly about the time that Charles I became King and his new Queen, Henrietta Maria, came over from France.

Men wore a *doublet* of silk or satin, sometimes with slashes in the material so that you could see the shirts they wore underneath the doublet. Sir Edmund Verney had a crimson satin doublet trimmed with gold lace, and also a purple satin one. The knee-length breeches were of silk or satin, too. They were often sewn or tied with ribbons down the sides of the legs to within five or six inches of the knee, and after that, they were open to show gay coloured linings or stockings. At the waist, instead of the belts or braces which men wear nowadays, there were ribbons. These ribbons were threaded through eyelet

Man's costume in the time of Charles I

holes on the waist of the doublet, and then the breeches
were fastened on to the doublet with bows of ribbon.

Their stockings were of knitted silk, and these were
held, where the breeches' legs overlapped the stockings,
by garters which were sashes of silk or ribbon wrapped
several times round the legs and then fastened in a bow.
Over these silk stockings, the men wore a second pair of

stockings called boot hose. These were made of a stronger material, perhaps of linen though sometimes they were also made of silk. The boot hose had fancy tops, sometimes embroidered, and sometimes edged with lace. The tops of the boot hose made a frill round the men's legs at the garters, and then the embroidered or lace tops fell in folds inside or over the loose tops of their boots. These stockings and boot hose were in every colour that you can think of: flesh-coloured, blue, green, yellow, scarlet, grey, black and white.

A fashionable boot

It was just as fashionable to wear boots as shoes: men could choose whichever they preferred. The King always wore boots, perhaps because he had had very weak legs as a child and he felt that he would not look so well in shoes. The shoes had square toes and round heels, and the toes were always decorated with a rosette of lace or ribbon. We are told that men sometimes paid as much as £5 (that is, in their money: it might mean £50 today) for the ornaments for their shoes. Boots reached to just below the knees, and they were so wide at the tops that they hung in folds. They were called 'bucket top boots'. The fashionable men at Court were not happy until they had their bucket top boots as wide as possible, with the fancy tops of their boot hose filling and spilling over the tops.

At their necks, men wore beautiful lace collars. Ralph Verney was wearing a lovely one when he had his portrait painted (see p. 4). Their cloaks were short, circular ones reaching just below the waist, and they liked to put their lace collars over the necks of their cloaks, so that you could see them. In the same way, they wore their lace collars over their buff coats when they were fighting in the war. The cloaks were usually lined to match their doublet or the colour of their hose. Sir Edmund Verney had a black cloak lined to match his doublet.

Men wore their hair long, touching their shoulders, and curled. Only a few Roundheads wore their hair so short that it just covered their ears. Mrs Hutchinson, although she and her husband were Roundheads, did not like the short hair style, and Colonel Hutchinson always wore his hair long. Many, like the King himself and Sir Edmund Verney, wore little pointed beards. We call these Van Dyck beards, because we see so many of these beards in portraits painted by Van Dyck. Other men, like Ralph Verney, John Hutchinson and Oliver Cromwell, were clean shaven.

At first, men's hats were soft felt hats, with coloured feathers sweeping from the brim on to their shoulders. Those were the hats which we always think of as 'Cavalier' hats. Later on, the fashionable hat had a high steep crown. These are the hats which we always think of as 'Roundhead' hats, but it is just that they were the fashionable hat to wear in the 1640s and 1650s. The King himself wore a high crowned hat at his trial.

The two styles of hat

People often think that the Puritans wore very plain dark clothes to show that they were different from the Cavaliers and that they scorned the King and the gay Court. This was true of some people, of course, but not of all who supported Parliament or could be called Puritans. Colonel Hutchinson usually wore clothes which were 'rich but grave, of sad-coloured cloth' (Mrs Hutchinson means that her husband wore rather dark-coloured cloth) but they were 'trimmed with gold'. His usual cloak was a 'scarlet cloak, very richly laced'. On one occasion, when most of Colonel Hutchinson's friends were wearing black suits, Harrison, one of the leading Parliamentary generals, wore a scarlet cloak and coat, both covered with gold and silver lace till the scarlet material could scarcely be seen through the lace. Ralph Verney, too, usually wore dark clothes: he had a slate-coloured suit.

What really mattered was whether you were rich or not, and whether you lived in the country or in London. There was not a great deal of difference between the clothes rich people wore, whether they were Cavaliers or Puritans. Though they may have worn rather darker and plainer suits in the years after the King's death and during the Commonwealth and the Protectorate, not every one did even then. In 1653, Ralph Verney's son, Edmund, wanted 150 yards of ribbon to trim his grey and black suit which he wore with scarlet stockings. When the boy went to stay in London in 1657 during the Protectorate, his uncle was horrified at the plain clothes he had and asked Ralph at once for permission to buy Edmund some clothes which would be 'fit for London'. Ralph agreed to this, and thought that 'Easter time is the fittest time to buy him clothes for then all fashions alter.'

For women, this was a period when they had very pretty clothes. Those women who were rich and could afford

Queen Henrietta Maria

the heavy silks and satins which they liked best, probably looked as beautiful as at any time in the history of women's fashions. The silks and satins were in the most lovely colours. If you can see the portrait of Queen Henrietta Maria in the National Portrait Gallery in London, you will see what a beautiful shade of olive green satin she was wearing when she had her portrait painted. Mary Verney, Ralph's wife, wore a pale blue dress with a white petticoat when she sat for her portrait.

The dresses had tight bodices and low, square necks.

The skirt was long and flowing, and at the back, it swept the ground almost into a train. This was pinned up when the wearer was walking out of doors. The skirt was usually divided up the front to show an elaborate petticoat, frilled with lace or ribbons and often embroidered.

Sometimes a lady's dress appeared to have three sleeves. The sleeves of her dress were fastened only at the shoulders and the cuffs, so that they fell open for the length of the sleeves. This meant you could see the sleeves of the fine linen smock which she wore under the dress. The sleeves of the smock were very full and were fastened at the elbows with ribbon or ornaments to make them balloon out. Yards and yards of ribbon covered the smock sleeves from shoulders to wrist. So, as the sleeves of the dress fell apart, you could see the wide sleeves of the smock and the oversleeves of ribbon. (Many of the men's doublets had this arrangement of sleeves and ribbons, too.)

Like the men, women wore collars and cuffs of lace or of the finest lawn trimmed with lace. Often the material was so fine that you could see through it to the low square neck of the dress below. This was just as true of the Puritan ladies, whom we might have expected to wear plainer clothes, as it was of the Royalist ladies at Court. There is a picture of Elizabeth, Cromwell's daughter, wearing a collar like this.

Lady with a fine collar

Plainer dress

Winter costume

Of course, ladies who were not wealthy enough to be dressed in such rich materials did wear plainer clothes made of darker and heavier materials. The dress might be made of wool with a linen collar, but even so, they wore much the same style of dress and their collars and aprons were edged with lace.

In cold weather, women wore cloaks with a hood, or else furs, and it was fashionable to carry a muff. In 1639, Lady Sussex wrote to Ralph Verney: 'I must trouble you to get me a handsome muff bought, a fashionable muff for someone as tall as your wife,' which was her way of getting Ralph to choose a muff as a present for Mary. Ladies often wore masks of velvet if they were out at nights, partly to protect their skins from the cold, for they were most anxious to keep their complexions fair, and partly because it was thought immodest for a lady not to cover her face when out at night. (This is the origin of the expression 'bare-faced' when you mean someone who is too bold.) The lady in the drawing, however, is evidently wearing her mask to protect her from the cold since she is so well wrapped up in her cloak and furs.

It was not only in the winter time that women tried to keep their skins smooth and white. In the summer, they often covered their heads with a veil so that they would not get sunburned. Apart from their hoods or veils, ladies had no special hats. If they wore a hat, perhaps when riding, then it was exactly like the men's soft hats which you have seen on p. 26.

Their shoes, too, were much the same as men's, with low heels and square toes. Women do not seem to have worn rosettes on their shoes, possibly because their feet could not be seen under their long dresses and so it was not worth spending as much on shoe ornaments as the men did.

The favourite hair style was to have the hair loosely but neatly arranged in curls which fell on either side of their faces, with perhaps a few longer curls falling on to their shoulders. At the back, the hair was arranged in a little bun: the curls were only at the sides. The Queen wore a little fringe, and so did many other ladies. On page 32 you can see that Mary Verney had a fringe, too.

All the women of this period wore pearls: that was their favourite jewellery. They wore strings of pearls round their necks, they had pearls sewn on to their dresses, they wore pearls in the ornaments which held the sleeves of their dresses together, and they often wore pearls in their

Mary Verney

hair. Apart from pearls, their favourite extravagance was lace or ribbons. You can well imagine how many yards of ribbon and lace were needed to tie up their sleeves and to ornament their dresses and petticoats. To give a friend some lengths of ribbon was a welcome present, just as much as to give them embroidered gloves or stockings. Ralph Verney sent one woman friend a present of fourteen pairs of gloves, twelve yards of scarlet ribbon and a pair of scarlet stockings. Ladies were always asking friends

Shopping scene

to buy ribbons for them and gave elaborate instructions of the kind and width they wanted. Lady Sussex asked Mary Verney to shop for her while Mary was in London with Ralph in 1639: 'Choose me out a lace which has but very little silver in it and not above a spangle or two: I would not have too heavy a lace about the breadth of a threepenny ribbon very little broader will be enough, some shadowed ribbon will be best of fourpenny breadth and I would have some little edging lace as slight as may be.' (Lady Sussex sounds as though she never stopped for breath when she talked: certainly her letters never had much punctuation in them.)

All the bright colours which both men and women wore disappeared completely if there was a death in the family. Then the pretty clothes were put away, and everyone went into deep mourning. Black was worn for three or four years after a parent died, while for a husband or wife it

33

was worn for much longer. Ralph Verney remained in mourning for Mary for the rest of his life. Everything Ralph wore after Mary's death was black: he had black cloth doublets, black breeches and cloak, black hats and hat bands, black taffeta garters and black ribbons for his shoes. He had black taffeta nightshirts, with black velvet night caps, and slippers of black velvet. Even his comb and brush were black.

Children, once they had grown out of their baby clothes, were dressed exactly the same as grown-ups. For the first few years, the little boys as well as the girls wore long dresses down to the ground. In the picture of Charles I's three eldest children, Charles Prince of Wales is old enough to be wearing a small version of a grown-up suit, the next child is wearing a long dress but it is James Duke of York, and then the child on the right *is* a girl, wearing a long dress and hair style just like her Mother's, the Queen. The boys' long dresses were called coats. Lady

Charles I's children

34

A little girl with her elder brother. How old do you think they are?

Sussex bought a sky blue satin coat for Ralph's son when he was four years old. Boys were about seven years of age when they began to wear grown up clothes instead of long coats, and there was usually great fun and fuss in the house when a boy was 'breeched'. Until they were about four or five, little boys wore a linen cap on their heads. The girls wore the same until they were about seven or eight. After that, the boys wore their hair long and in curls, and the girls wore a ribbon or pearls in their hair, so that they all looked like miniature grown-ups.

Once the war started, men and women, boys and girls, must have had fewer new clothes because of all the difficulties which war brings. There were taxes to be paid to

35

Parliament if they lived in an area controlled by Parliament, or money to be given to the King if they were Royalists, and their homes were likely to be looted by troops of either side. In all the Verney letters, there are complaints of being poor because people would not pay their debts or pay their rents during the unsettled times. After the war, the Cavaliers had heavy fines to pay, while everyone in the country had to pay more in taxes to the Commonwealth and the Protectorate than ever they had paid to Charles I. Nevertheless, people still went on minding about fashion, and Paris, even in those days, was considered to have the smartest fashions. Among all the anxieties of the war, when Mary and Ralph were unhappy and poor exiles in France, one of their friends wrote to Mary to say 'I hear you are in Paris, I will make no new clothes until you direct me.' She then went on to ask Mary to buy her four or five yards of coloured satin so that she could make a new petticoat (this would be for the fancy petticoat which was part of her dress) and she asked Mary to spend thirty shillings 'on any pretty thing for my head' which probably means that she wanted a new pearl ornament or a knot of ribbons for her hair.

So, even in the darkest days of the war, people still minded about their clothes and wanted to look smart. But now it is time to find out why the war started and what happened to the Verneys during those bad

An embroidered linen nightcap days.

4

Why King and Parliament Quarrelled

From the very beginning of his reign in 1625, Charles I quarrelled with his Parliaments. As King, he really did not have enough money to govern the country properly, but Parliament was becoming more and more unwilling to vote him sufficient money in taxes. The King thought that he had the right to decide nearly everything and all Parliament had to do was to vote him the taxes to allow him to rule. Many members of the House of Commons, however, thought that they should have some control over the way their money was spent.

Charles I's father, James I, believed that a good King was 'ordained of his people, having received from God a burden of government'. He had taught his son this. It was a King's duty to rule well, but his subjects were bound to obey him without question: if a King ruled them badly, then he had to answer to God for his faults but not to his people. Many of his subjects who sat in the Parliaments, of course, did not agree with this.

Parliament, then as now, was made up of two Houses, the House of Lords and the House of Commons. The House of Commons, however, did not represent everyone as it does today. The people who sat in it were mainly well-to-do people. They were country gentlemen or rich merchants or lawyers. These were all important people in

37

The House of Commons in 1651

the country and naturally they did not agree with the
King's belief that he had a Divine Right to rule them
without being questioned by them. They felt that if they
were to pay with their taxes for the King's decisions, such
as whether the King should go to war with France or
Spain, then they wanted to be able to discuss it in Parliament and to have some say in matters of importance.

So in the first two years of his reign, in 1625 and 1626,
Charles quarrelled with and dismissed two Parliaments.
Then he tried to raise money without the consent of
Parliament. When he was at war with France and Spain in
1627, for example, each county was simply ordered to pay
him a certain amount of money. In the letters of the Verney

family, we read that the gentlemen of Buckinghamshire were ordered to give the King £3,052 and to lend him half as much again. All over the country there were protests and grumbles about this, and while most men ended by paying their share of their county's money, some gentlemen like Sir John Eliot and John Hampden refused to pay and were put in prison for it.

In 1628, Charles was forced to call Parliament again to try to persuade them to vote him some money in taxes. Sir Edmund Verney was elected as M.P. for Aylesbury for this Parliament, so he rode up to London for the meeting of Parliament. Both Houses began by debating their grievances that the King should have tried to raise money without the consent of Parliament. Together, they forced the King to accept what they called the Petition of Right. This said that in future no man should be asked to pay

Charles I in the House of Lords, when state robes were worn

any gift, loan or tax to the King without the consent of Parliament. Then the House of Commons, led by Sir John Eliot, went on further to attack the King. Charles ordered the Speaker to stop the debate but some M.P.s held the Speaker in his chair and would not let him leave the House of Commons until they had finished their speeches. Afterwards, the King put Sir John Eliot in prison again along with some other M.P.s for their share in this.

After that angry ending to Parliament in 1629, Charles tried for eleven years to rule without Parliament. In many ways, he tried to be a good King. From his portraits, it looks as though he was a very delicate man. He was fond of music and of painting: he bought many beautiful pictures. He had the ceiling of the newly finished Banqueting Hall of his Palace at Whitehall painted by Rubens, the greatest painter of the day, and you can still see this. His subjects, however, were much less interested in the elegance of the King's Court than in the ways he tried to get money from them.

We can see some of those ways through Sir Edmund Verney. When Charles became King, he rewarded Sir Edmund's faithful service to him from his boyhood by making him the Knight Marshal of the Palace at Whitehall. This meant that he was responsible for seeing that the Palace and the district around it was kept free from vagabonds and from any disturbances. To do this, Sir Edmund paid men to ride about like policemen and arrest any offenders. The King was so short of money that he paid Sir Edmund to do this, not with a salary, but by granting him what were called *patents*. Sir Edmund, for example, had a share in the patent for inspecting all the tobacco in the country. He had one for inspecting all the woollen yarn before it could be made into cloth. He had a share in another for licensing hackney coaches (which

40

were then new in London) before they could go on the streets. The King claimed the right to these patents because it was his duty as King to see that tobacco and woollen yarn were of good quality before they could be sold, and that hackney coaches were safe before they could be hired. In fact, of course, the patents were just another way that the King used to get money, and the extra money they brought in went to men like Sir Edmund as a way of paying them for their work. Parliament had attacked the claim of the Crown to do this since Queen Elizabeth's days, and it had forced James I in 1624 to promise not to levy what were then called *monopolies*. Charles I called them patents instead of monopolies—and continued to raise money in this way.

But the scheme for raising money for the King which made most people angry was one called Ship Money. This was another tax from Queen Elizabeth's reign to provide money for the Navy, and Charles I revived it. In Queen Elizabeth's day only the towns on the coast had had to pay it, for they needed the protection of the Navy most. Charles I made everyone pay it. Immediately, those counties which had never paid Ship Money before, protested and said that he should have asked Parliament first. In many ways, this was perhaps the fairest of all Charles I's ways of trying to raise money, and he really did spend the money he got from it on ships for the Navy. One ship which was built with this money was the greatest ship of the day, 'The Sovereign of the Seas'. Nevertheless, many landowners refused to pay Ship Money.

The King decided to prosecute one man in order to make an example of him to all the others who would not pay. The man who was charged was John Hampden of Buckinghamshire, for refusing to pay twenty shillings on some land he owned at Stoke Mandeville. John Hampden could well have afforded to pay this money, but just

John Hampden

as he had refused to pay the money the King had asked for in 1627, so now he refused to pay Ship Money because the King had not got the consent of Parliament. After long arguments at his trial, seven of the King's judges decided that John Hampden was guilty and must pay the money, but five judges, even though they were the King's judges, voted for John Hampden. One of the judges who thought that John Hampden was right to claim that Parliament should be asked, said: 'Royal power is to be used in cases of necessity and imminent danger, but in a time of peace and no extreme necessity, legal courses must be used and not royal power.'

There was another great difference between the King and the kind of people who sat in Parliament, apart from all this problem of money. This was religion. The Reformation was not so far away that men had ceased to fight about religion. They had not yet learned that people of different faiths, or of no belief at all, can live together in peace. It was felt necessary then that everyone living in a country should belong to one Church. Wars were still being fought in Europe about this, and English sympathies were with the Protestant countries. Many in England felt that the Reformation here had not been Protestant enough, and they wanted something more like the Nonconformist Churches of today. Charles I, and William Laud who was the Archbishop of Canterbury, wanted the Church of England to be a dignified Church: they wanted the churches to be beautiful with fine *vestments* and handsome furnishings, they wanted the services to be conducted well, and they believed that the Church of England with the King at its head, and then the archbishops, bishops and clergy was the right and only possible Church. By Charles I's day, however, there were many who wanted the Church of England to be changed. These are the people who are known as Puritans. Some wanted more preaching and less service: others thought that in the early Church there had been no archbishops and bishops, but that every congregation was its own church, and that was what they wanted in their own day. Because the Queen, Henrietta Maria, was a Roman Catholic, they thought that the King was secretly planning to return to Roman Catholicism: in fact, the King was a sincere member of the Church of England and had no intention of doing this. Archbishop Laud punished severely anyone who spoke against the King's and his own policy in the Church. John Prynne, for example, had his ears cut off for writing against a bishop.

In Scotland, dislike of the bishops was even stronger than in England. Charles I and Archbishop Laud decided to force the Church of Scotland to become more like the

Church of England, and to have services and a Prayer Book like the English one. Sunday, 28 July 1637, was the day fixed for the introduction of a new Prayer Book in Scotland. The congregation in St Giles Cathedral in Edinburgh shouted and threw their Bibles and stools at the minister when he began the new service that day. Much the same sort of thing happened in other churches in Scotland.

Before long, the Scots had drawn up, and many had signed, what they called a National *Covenant* to oppose the King's policy in the Church: those who signed became known as Covenanters. Most of the Scots prepared to fight the King if he should force his will on them.

William Laud, Archbishop of Canterbury

5

The Quarrel Between King and Parliament Grows Worse

In February 1639, Sir Edmund Verney was summoned to attend the King 'upon a Royal journey to York'. This was the King gathering an army together to march against his Scottish subjects. Sir Edmund did not approve of what the King was doing, but nevertheless he obeyed. He evidently feared the worst, for he made his will before he left London with the King. When they reached York, they were greeted with bad news. Sir Edmund wrote to Ralph from York to say that 'the King has been basely betrayed: the two castles of Edinburgh and Dumbarton are yielded up without one blow, and yet they were both provided for so well, as they were *impregnable*'. The loyal town of Aberdeen, to which the King had intended to send his fleet, was also in the hands of the Covenanters.

The trouble was that the King had not been told—or rather, had not listened to the few who had told him—how strongly the Scots felt about his Church plans. The governor of the castle at Dalkeith, where the Crown Jewels of Scotland were kept, refused to hand over the keys and surrender to the Covenanters, but he hinted to them that there were other ways into the castle—so the Crown Jewels of Scotland were now in Edinburgh in the Covenanters' hands.

D   45

The King and his army made their way north to Berwick. The Scots sent a letter to the King, saying that they meant no injury to him, but 'they have often presented their grievances to his Majesty and by reason of some ill-minded men can get no answer'. Sir Edmund thought their letter was a good one, but he told Ralph that others with the King thought that it was 'full of insolence'. Sir Edmund grew even more depressed about the King's chances of success against the Scots. He wrote to Ralph: 'Our army is but weak: our purse is weaker still, and if we fight with these forces we shall have our throats cut, and to delay fighting long we cannot for want of money to keep our army together.'

When the two armies faced each other near Berwick, the King realized, too, that his straggling soldiers were no match for the well armed and well drilled Scots who knew what they were prepared to fight for. Messengers rode to and fro between the King and the Scottish leaders. Sir Edmund was one of these messengers; he wrote to Ralph that he had talked to one 'understanding Scottishman' who 'is confident that nothing will satisfy them but the taking away all bishops, and I dare say the King will never yield to that, so we must be miserable'. Because he realized that he could not fight the Scots, the King played for time by promising them that he would come to Edinburgh later in the year for a meeting of the Scottish Parliament and the Scottish Church Assembly. Both sides then agreed to disband their armies. The King rode back to London: Sir Edmund said that they did the 260 miles in four days. The Assembly of the Church of Scotland, when it met, refused to have bishops in the Church in Scotland or to accept the new Prayer Book. The Scottish Parliament, too, defied the King.

Charles then called home to England from Ireland his

Thomas Wentworth (Lord Strafford)

most capable servant, Thomas Wentworth. He had been Deputy Governor in Ireland since 1632. Wentworth, soon to be made Lord Strafford, advised the King to be firm with the Scots and to call the English Parliament to vote money for a war against Scotland. He obviously did not realize how strongly people were against the King's plans in England and, still more, in Scotland.

Charles I accepted Strafford's advice, and on 13 April 1640, Parliament met for the first time since 1629. Sir Edmund Verney was elected as M.P. for Wycombe, and Ralph was elected as M.P. for Aylesbury, so father and son were together in the House of Commons, sitting for towns in their county of Buckinghamshire. Immediately Parliament met, the Commons refused to vote any money to the King and, led by John Pym, they brought up all their old grievances against the King: Ship Money, the

Church, the behaviour of the King's judges. Charles I tried to give way a little: he offered to abolish Ship Money if only the Commons would vote him taxes instead. Pym and the other leaders paid no attention to this; they voted that all their complaints must be settled first. In desperation, the King ended the Parliament on 5 May. Because it had only lasted for three weeks, it is called the Short Parliament.

By this time, the Covenanters were already marching south again, ready to fight the King. Charles I forced the City of London to lend him money, and he raised some by selling patents. Then, with the promise of some troops from Ireland by Lord Strafford, he got an army together to meet the Scots. Young Mun Verney was with the King's army this time. He found it badly equipped and not fit to fight the Scots, just as his father had felt the year before. The Royal army was badly beaten at Newburn, near Newcastle upon Tyne. Mun wrote home to say: 'That we were beaten, you have heard. The business was very ill-managed by some, for we had neither cannon nor ammunition with us, but went like lambs to the slaughter,' and since then 'we have been hastily employed running away'. The King had to make peace with the Scots after this defeat: he agreed to pay them £850 a day until their grievances were settled.

This meant that Charles *had* to call Parliament in order to pay the Scots. He could not collect this amount of money in the various ways that had let him manage without Parliament up till then. The new Parliament met on 3 November 1640. Because, in theory at least, it lasted until 1660, it is known as the Long Parliament, and it is one of the most important in our history. Sir Edmund Verney was again elected for Wycombe and Ralph for Aylesbury, so once more father and son were together. Mun wrote to his father and brother to congratulate them on being elected, and to remind them that he, and the rest of the army, had not been paid since they had been called to fight the Scots in May.

At once the new House of Commons started making the old complaints. John Pym summed them all up in a speech: the freedom of Parliament had been attacked because the King had ruled without one: only clergy who preached the Divine authority of the King were approved of in the Church: the liberty of the subject had been attacked by unlawful taxes.

All the blame for the King's way of ruling during the past years was put on Lord Strafford and Archbishop Laud. They were arrested by Parliament and sent to the Tower of London as prisoners. Lord Strafford was accused of treason by the House of Commons. The only real evidence that the Commons had against Lord Strafford for treason was that when he had been called back from Ireland to advise the King about the Scots, he had said that he had an army in Ireland which could be used to 'reduce this Kingdom'. John Pym insisted that by 'this Kingdom' Strafford meant England, and that he was therefore advising the King to fight his English subjects. Strafford denied this: he had meant Scotland by 'this Kingdom'. He defended himself well against all the charges that he had been a dangerous adviser to the King.

It looked as though Lord Strafford's defence of himself would be successful, and so the Commons passed a *Bill of Attainder* against him. This means that Parliament simply *said* that Strafford *was* guilty, and there was no need to prove it. Ralph Verney kept notes of this debate and of the number who voted in it. (This was forbidden in Parliament, and Ralph must have kept his notes hidden

The trial of Strafford in the House of Lords

in some way: perhaps under a hat.) According to Ralph's notes, 204 members in the Commons voted against Strafford and only 39 for him, while in the Lords 25 voted against Strafford, 19 for him and many did not vote at all. So it is clear that many M.P.s hated Strafford and thought he was guilty of treason, even if they could not prove it, and very few M.P.s dared to support one of the King's most able servants. Ralph obviously thought that Strafford was guilty, for he wrote down Lord Falkland's speech against Strafford as though he approved of its way of explaining the difficulties of proving the Earl guilty. 'How many hair's-breadths make a tall man and how many make a little man, no man can well say, yet we know a tall man when we see him from a low man, so tis in this, how many illegal acts make a treason it is certainly not well known, but yet we know it well when we see it.' We see from the letters written to Ralph about this time, that many of the Verneys' friends were against Strafford, too: Lady Sussex wrote, 'Yon great lord, I hope he will come to the honour of beheading: if he escapes he will do more ill than ever was done', and 'I pray God your houses may agree, and that they will make an end of this great lord.'

At first the King would not accept the Bill of Attainder against Strafford: he had promised his servant that he would see that Parliament could not harm him. But the London mobs shouted round the Palace of Whitehall, terrifying the King and still more the Queen. Charles was desperate to know what to do. Lord Strafford sent a message that he would willingly die if it would help the situation, so in the end, the King agreed to Strafford's execution. In later life, and when it came to the day of his own execution, Charles was to say that all his sufferings had come upon him as a just punishment for this.

On the day Lord Strafford was executed, in May 1641, the King had to accept a bill that this Parliament, which was attacking him and his servants so fiercely, could not be ended except with its own consent, so the King could not dismiss it as he had done his earlier Parliaments. Other laws followed one after the other to prevent the King from ever again being able to rule the country without a Parliament.

When the House of Commons went on to discuss religious matters, many members who had been united in opposing the King's methods of ruling the country would not agree with any change in the Church of England. Ralph Verney, however, agreed with John Pym and others who wanted to have a Church of England without Bishops. 'We shall do our best to abolish them utterly as the Scots

51

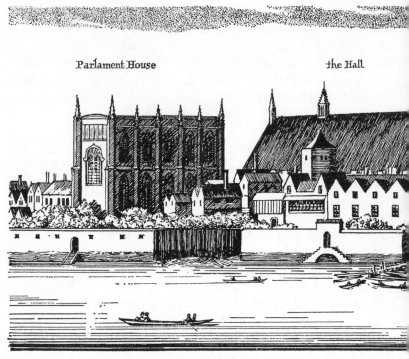

Parlament House   the Hall

Westminster in the seventeenth century

have done,' Ralph wrote. A group of M.P.s introduced a
bill in which they asked that bishops should be removed
from the Church of England 'root and branch'. Many
M.P.s would not agree with this, and they opposed the
Root and Branch Bill. They were the beginnings of a party
which would, in the end, support the King, not because of
the way he had ruled, but in order to save the Church of
England and to prevent it from being turned into a Presbyterian Church.

When John Pym realized that the House of Commons
was splitting in two, although it had been so united in
attacking the King up till then, he tried to draw the

the Abbey

M.P.s together again with a long statement—a Grand *Remonstrance*—of all their past grievances against the King. This only made the quarrel between King and Parliament more bitter, but worse was yet to come. While the debates were going on, news reached London that the Irish had risen in revolt against England. On 7 December 1641, Sir Arthur Haslerig, one of Pym's chief supporters, proposed that the army and navy should be under the control of Parliament: Parliament, not the King, would be in control of the troops to be sent to Ireland. The King felt that he just could not agree to this: he had given in sufficiently to this House of Commons. Without the right to command the army and navy, he would have no royal power left at all. He decided to make a stand against this latest proposal by charging John Pym, John Hampden, Arthur Haslerig, Denzil Hollis and William Strode of the House of Commons, and Lord Mandeville of the House of Lords, with treason because they were the leaders of this movement to take away his powers from him. The King ordered the House of Commons to send the five M.P.s to him, but the House refused, saying that this would break the privilege of Members of Parliament to speak with absolute freedom on any subject.

On the morning of 4 January 1642, the five members of the House of Commons were warned to go into hiding. Obviously Charles I's plans had leaked out. It is thought that one of the Queen's ladies gave John Pym a hint of what was being planned at Court, and that the French Ambassador warned him, too. Soon after the five M.P.s had gone to hide in the City of London, the King came into the House of Commons with his guards. Ralph Verney was in the House, and his notes tell us what happened. The King left his guards outside the Chamber, and he came into the Commons, taking his hat off to show some respect for the M.P.s. The King went up to the Speaker's chair and stood on the step. 'And, after he had looked a great while, he told us that he would not break our privileges: he came for the five gentlemen.' Then the King 'called Mr. Pym and Mr. Hollis by name, but no answer came. Then he asked the Speaker if they were there, or where they were. Upon that, the Speaker fell on his knees and desired his excuse, for he was a servant of the House, and had neither eyes, nor tongue, to see or say but what they commanded him. Then the King told him that he thought his eyes were as good as his, and then said that his birds were flown. The King told the Members of Parliament who were present that he expected them to send the five members to him. 'He assured us that they would have a fair trial' and so he went away.

From that time onwards, there was little hope of settling the quarrel between the King and his Parliament, for neither side trusted the other. On 10 January 1642, the King left for Hampton Court and then Windsor Castle. He was never to return to London again until he was brought back as a prisoner. The five members of Parliament sailed back from the City of London to Westminster on the day after the King left, and crowds cheered their barge all the way along the river.

Men began to collect their arms and to prepare to fight. Even so, many hoped that it still would not come to a war. Lady Sussex wrote to Ralph: 'I pray God that there may be agreement betwixt the King and his people, and that poor England may have some help.' At times, even she, who was usually a great supporter of Parliament and had wanted Strafford beheaded, thought that Parliament was asking too much of the King. She wrote to Ralph on one occasion: 'I am sorry that your Parliament goes on in such a violent way. I pray God we do not all suffer from it.' One of Ralph's relatives wrote to him: 'I am in such a rage with Parliament as nothing will *pacify* me, for they promised that all should be well if my Lord Strafford's head were off, and since then nothing is better.'

At the end of February, the Queen sailed for Holland, taking her jewels with her to try to get money for the King. In April, the King tried to enter the town of Hull to take charge of the seaport which would let him keep in touch with the Queen and give him the store of ammunition there, but the Governor, Sir John Hotham, closed the gates of the town and would not let the King enter. By June, Sir Edmund wrote home to Claydon to arrange about the house in case war came and to say which servants and horses he would need.

Both King and Parliament sent out orders for men and ammunitions to support them. In some counties, Parliament's orders were obeyed: in others, it was the King's command which was obeyed. In Nottingham, when the King's men arrived to take possession of the county's store of ammunition, John Hutchinson tried to stop them from taking it, saying that it had been collected for the protection of the county and ought not to be taken away by anyone, even the King. One of the King's officers ordered his arrest. John Hutchinson escaped by the back door of the house just as the Royal troops entered the house to seize him. His wife, Lucy, stayed behind to face the troops to give her husband the chance to escape, and when the officer in charge of the soldiers came into the house—it was her own brother, Allan! Here was one of the first reminders, before war had started, that brother and sister would be on different sides. Allan Apsley saw that no harm came to his sister until he had to move on with his men.

So even before the war had been declared there was trouble all over the country. Already, the two sides were beginning to use the nicknames of 'Roundhead' and 'Cavalier'. When the King's men were taking the ammunition from Nottingham, one of them said to John Hutchinson that he wished his musket was loaded and he 'hoped that the day would soon come for all roundheads such as he', although, in fact, John Hutchinson had long hair and was not at all a 'roundhead'.

Cavalier simply means a horseman, but at that time the word had an ugly meaning: it was the word used for Spanish troops who had a reputation for cruelty and brutality. When the Parliament's supporters used it of the

King's men, they were implying that the Cavaliers were brutal and cruel. Roundhead was the name given to the supporters of Parliament, partly because the apprentices of London had to wear their hair cut short and it was they who had caused much of the disturbances round the Palace of Whitehall at the time of Strafford's trial, and partly because some of the Puritan supporters of Parliament kept their hair short to show that they were not vain about their appearance. Mrs Hutchinson did not like this short hair, even though these men were on the side her husband supported. She thought the short hair was 'ridiculous to behold', and she was very proud of her husband's 'fine thick set head of hair' which she thought was 'a great ornament to him'. She tells us, too, that the fashion among Parliament's supporters for wearing hair short died out so soon that three or four years later no stranger could have told why they were called 'Roundheads'.

Still, the nicknames caught on, so that we still remember those who supported King Charles in the Civil War as 'Cavaliers' and those who supported Parliament as 'Roundheads'.

6

The War

Nottingham was probably chosen by the King as the place at which he would make his declaration of war because it is a convenient meeting place for the Midlands, and because it was a district where he had many supporters. Lucy Hutchinson tells us that most of her husband's relations and friends in Nottinghamshire were for the King, although most of what she calls 'the middle sort' were for Parliament.

It was a miserably cold wet day in Nottingham on 22 August 1642. The King's standard was an enormously heavy flag which took twenty men to steady it. It was not the one which would be carried into battle with the King, but a special one for the occasion. On the standard were the King's coat of arms, a crown, and a hand pointing to the crown with the words 'Give Caesar his due'. This means that Charles claimed that, as a King, he was entitled to all the powers which he believed belonged to a King but which Parliament was taking away from him. With the King that day in Nottingham was his eldest son Charles, Prince of Wales who was then twelve years old, his nephew Prince Rupert who was twenty-three years of age and who had come from Germany to help his uncle, about 300 horse and 800 foot soldiers, and a number of gentlemen and nobles. Altogether, there was a crowd of

Prince Rupert

about 2,000 gathered round the standard. The herald could barely read the King's message to his people because Charles had altered it so much, but when he was finished reading it, there was a shout of 'God save the King' and men threw their hats in the air while the drums were beaten and the trumpets were blown.

Sir Edmund Verney was one of those at Nottingham with the King that day. He was made the King's Standard Bearer. From then on, it would be his duty to guard the King's standard and to carry it into battle wherever the King might be. He vowed 'by the grace of God, they that would *wrest* the standard from my hand must first wrest my soul from my body'. Yet Sir Edmund was not happy about this declaration of war. He told Edward Hyde, who later became Lord Clarendon and wrote the history of the war, 'My condition is much worse than yours. You have the satisfaction that you are in the right: that the King ought not to grant what is required of him, so you do your duty and your business together. But for my part, I do not like the quarrel and do heartily wish that the King would yield and consent to what they desire, so my conscience is only concerned in love and gratitude to follow my master.' He felt that 'I have eaten his bread and served him nearly thirty years, and will not do so base a thing as to foresake him,' but, he added, 'I will deal freely with you, I have no reverence for the Bishops for whom this quarrel subsists.' So, for Sir Edmund, it was a mixture of loyalty to the King and the fact that he owed so much to the King which meant that he was at Nottingham that day and that he would fight for Charles. It is clear that he felt that the King and Parliament were really fighting over religion. Yet though Sir Edmund did not think the King was right, he was very sad when his son Ralph decided not to join him in the King's army but to stay in Parliament.

There were many men, like Sir Edmund, who decided to fight for the King out of loyalty or gratitude. Many more ended by supporting the King although they had been his bitterest opponents in Parliament so long as he had tried to rule by himself. Edward Hyde, for example, was a lawyer who had attacked the King's courts in Parliament, but he felt that once the King had accepted the laws which abolished those courts, then Parliament had gone far enough and so he fought for the King. Lord Falkland had voted against the King in Parliament until men like John Pym began to attack the Church of England. Lord Falkland was one of many who joined the

Royal army, not to save the King but to save the Church of England from being altered by Parliament. Out of the 552 M.P.s who had helped to limit the powers of the King through the Acts of the Long Parliament between 1640 and 1642, more than two-fifths of them ended by supporting the King.

So, for some people, it looks as though one of the reasons for the Civil War was religion. Yet John Hutchinson, who was one who could be called a Puritan, did not think that the real quarrel between the King and Parliament was over the Church. His wife, Lucy, tells us that when the revolt in Ireland began in November 1641, John Hutchinson read all that he could about King and Parliament. He decided that it was the way the King had been ruling which really mattered, and so he decided to fight for Parliament. His father, Sir Thomas Hutchinson, was an M.P. who did not want the quarrel between King and Parliament to end in fighting, but when his two sons decided to fight for Parliament, he helped them to buy arms and gave them money to pay for troops to serve with them.

Those who decided to fight for Parliament, whether it was for political or religious reasons, would not admit at first that they were fighting the King himself. They said that they were fighting to save the King from all his mistakes and from his bad advisers. So the Parliamentary army was raised 'for the safety of the King's person, the defence of both Houses of Parliament, preserving true religion, the laws, the liberty and peace of the Kingdom'. When John Hampden was killed fighting for Parliament, he was wearing round his neck a pendant on which was written: 'Against my King I do not fight, but for my King and Kingdom's right.'

Gradually, and for many different reasons, men took sides

61

Robert Devereux, Earl of Essex

against each other. There was no clear-cut division between them. On the whole, more lords fought for the King than for Parliament, but many fought for Parliament. The Parliamentary army was first commanded by the Earl of Essex and the Earl of Manchester. Nor was there anything more than a rough geographical division of the country. Support for Parliament was strongest in the south and east of England, while those who supported the King were strongest in the north of England, in the west midlands and the south-west, and in Wales. In every district, however, there were many on the other side. What really mattered was that Parliament could collect more money from the parts of the country mainly on its side than the King could collect from the parts which supported him. Sussex, for example, is usually counted as a Parliamentary county but there were many loyal supporters of the King there. What mattered was that the Parliamentary majority controlled most of the Sussex iron works, which meant that Parliament could get its guns made at home while the King had to have most of his brought in from abroad. The Navy, on which the King had spent the Ship Money which had given him so much trouble, declared almost completely for Parliament: only one ship supported the King. Only two seaports, Newcastle upon Tyne and King's Lynn, declared for the King. Thus the King had difficulty in getting from abroad the supplies he needed for his army, and although many of his supporters gave him money and melted down their silver to help him, he could never raise as much money as his enemies. His main hope was to win the war quickly.

At first, the chief problem for both sides was to get an army together at all. From Nottingham, the King went to Shrewsbury, and from the loyal district there and from Wales, he gathered together an army of about 10,000 foot soldiers and 2,000 horse. He was cheered by the news that Cornwall under Sir Ralph Hopton and the north of England under the Earl of Newcastle had declared for him, and he began marching through Wolverhampton and Kenilworth on his way to London. In the meanwhile, the Earl of Essex had gathered together an army of about 15,000 men for Parliament, mainly from London and from the recruits he had got at Coventry and Northampton. Towards the end of October, the two armies were near each other in Warwickshire. So slowly did news travel in those days, that although it was two months since war had been declared, a man called Richard Shuckburgh was out hunting when he was surprised to meet the King's army marching along the road on its way to meet Lord Essex's army. He rushed home, collected his tenants together, and joined the King in time for the battle of Edgehill the next day.

On 23 October 1642, the first great battle of the Civil War took place on what must be the loveliest battlefield in England, overlooking the fields and woods of Warwickshire. Edgehill is a great crest of land: from the top, the ground falls steeply to the countryside below. Charles's army camped for the night of the 22nd on the top of the hill, and with the daylight, they moved down the hill to the lower slopes. Lord Essex quickly got his men out of their marching order into formation for battle, but the Royalists had so strong a position on the hillside that they waited for the Parliamentary army to make the first move. Instead, Lord Essex waited, too, so for some hours the two armies stood ready and watching each other. Neither army had any uniform as yet and men were wearing their ordinary clothes, so the King's soldiers wore red scarves and the other side orange ones to help them to pick out their own side once the battle began. The King, wearing armour with a black velvet cloak over it and a velvet covered helmet, moved about his men to encourage them. He said: 'Your King bids you be courageous and Heaven make you victorious.' It was while each side was waiting that Sir Jacob Astley in the King's army said a prayer which we still remember: 'Lord, Thou knowest how busy I must be this day: if I forget Thee, do not Thou forget me.'

In the afternoon, quite suddenly, Prince Rupert began the battle by charging the opposite cavalry: he took the Parliamentary horsemen facing him completely by surprise and swept them off the field. Lord Wilmot with the King's cavalry on the left side of the Royal army was less successful against the Parliamentary cavalry facing him, while the infantry in the middle on both sides fought bravely and stubbornly. By six o'clock there were thousands of men dead on the field and both sides had stopped fighting. Somewhere among the dead lay Sir Edmund Verney. A group of Parliamentary cavalry had made a strong attack to try to capture the King's standard from him. Sir Edmund killed several of them as he fought to defend the standard until he himself was killed. To get the standard away from his dead hand, the attacking soldiers had to cut his hand off, and so the promise which

Sir Edmund had made at Nottingham two months before had been kept. As the battle drew near its end, a young cavalry officer called John Smith managed to recapture the King's standard and galloped back to the King with it. One story says that he picked up an orange scarf from a dead Roundhead, put it on, and so got through the enemy forces. For this, the King knighted him on the spot.

Both sides claimed Edgehill as a victory, but, as Mrs Hutchinson wrote: 'It is not yet agreed who gained the victory that day', for both sides had lost many men. At least the King remained on the battlefield while Lord Essex and his men left. One officer with the Parliamentary force had been at his first battle that day, and had seen how hard his side would have to learn to fight if they were to win. His name was Oliver Cromwell, and he said to his cousin, John Hampden, about the way the Parliamentary soldiers behaved: 'Do you think the spirits of such base and mean fellows will ever be able to encounter gentlemen that have honour, courage and resolution in them? . . . You must get men of a spirit that is like to go as far as a gentleman will, or else I am sure you will be beaten still.' So he went home to raise in his own area of East Anglia an army which would be able to beat the King's army.

After the battle of Edgehill, the King made for Oxford, which became his headquarters for the rest of the war. In November, his troops marched towards London to try to take the city. As Prince Rupert got near London, however, every available man poured out of London to oppose the King's forces. When the Royalists got to Turnham Green, they found 24,000 Londoners waiting to fight them. They were so outnumbered that it would have been madness to fight, and so they withdrew to Oxford, while the house-wives of London sent out their Sunday dinners to feed the men who had turned back the King's army by just facing it in such large numbers. The King never got so near London again during the war.

As the year 1643 began, it still looked hopeful for the King. The Queen returned from Holland with money and guns to help him, though she had had an exciting time reaching England: Parliamentary ships chased her into Bridlington and fired their guns at her party. The Earl of Newcastle was in control of the north of England and had garrisoned towns like York, Pontefract and Newark for the King. Sir Ralph Hopton defeated a Parliamentary army at Braddock Down in Cornwall on 19 January 1643.

It was decided that the three Royal armies should move in on London. The plan was that the northern army should move south from Yorkshire, the Cornish army should come eastwards till it was south of London, and the King should bring his army from Oxford. In this way, they would be able to encircle London. It was a good plan, but it did not work. The Earl of Newcastle dared not leave the north until he had defeated Hull. Sir Ralph Hopton got as far as Sussex, but he could not risk all his forces while towns like Plymouth held out for Parliament. The King decided to attack Gloucester with his army from Oxford because its Parliamentary garrison was holding up his forces in the west which he needed badly, but the town managed to hold out till it was relieved by the Earl of Essex from London, though it had only three barrels of powder left by the time the Parliamentary army rescued it. A big battle was fought at Newbury on 20 September 1643 when the King's army from Oxford met the Earl of Essex's army on its way back to London from Gloucester, but again it was a battle which neither side could claim as a victory.

Both sides then began to look for allies to help them. The King turned to Ireland, and made a treaty with the Irish

66

leaders who were still fighting the rebellion which had helped to touch off the Civil War. This released English soldiers who could come back to join the King, but this 'Irish army' was very little help to him. Soon after it landed in England, it was defeated at Nantwich in Cheshire before it could join any of the King's main armies, and more than half the survivors changed sides and fought for Parliament.

Parliament turned to the Scots for help. In return for an army of 20,000 men from Scotland, Parliament promised to make England a Presbyterian country. Every M.P., and every person of importance in the areas controlled by Parliament, had to agree to this and take the oath of the Solemn League and Covenant. John Pym arranged this treaty with the Scots: it was almost the last service he could do for the cause he believed in, as he died soon afterwards. Ralph Verney, who had stayed in Parliament as an M.P. even though his father had been killed fighting for the King and his three brothers were now with the Royal forces, was one of those who did not agree with John Pym about this and he would not take the oath. He still would not fight for the King, but he could no longer agree with Parliament, and so he went into exile in France rather than join either side.

The Scots crossed the Border early in January 1644, and their well trained and experienced troops helped to defeat the King. On 2 July 1644, Prince Rupert's army of about 17,000 men met the combined Parliamentary army of the Earl of Manchester and the Scottish forces under Alexander Leslie, Earl of Leven, which together numbered about 27,000 men. The two armies faced each other all day at Marston Moor near York. Prince Rupert decided to place his own cavalry on the right wing where they would have to fight Oliver Cromwell, for by then he

Drawn up for battle

knew that Cromwell's troops from East Anglia were the best in the Parliamentary forces. By seven o'clock in the evening, Prince Rupert decided that there was not going to be a battle that night, and he went to the back of the army to have his supper. The Earl of Newcastle went to his coach to smoke a pipe, while the Cavalier soldiers tried to get some rest for they had all had a hard time, some besieged in York, and the others marching with Rupert to relieve the town. Suddenly, as a thunderstorm began at half-past seven, the whole line of the Parliamentary army moved. Prince Rupert rushed to rally his men who were taken completely off their guard. Cromwell was wounded, and it was mainly the Scots who defeated Prince Rupert's cavalry facing them, but Cromwell was able to take over and to lead his troops round the back of the Royalist infantry to defeat the Royalist cavalry on the other wing. The infantry fought stubbornly on both sides till many of the King's men were killed or surrendered. The Earl of Newcastle's men fought on till few were left alive. The whole battle was over in two hours. Thousands of the King's supporters had been killed in the fighting. After the battle of Marston Moor there was really no hope for the King's side in the north of England. Parliament was in control.

Even at this stage, however, all did not seem lost for the

King. The Marquis of Montrose began fighting for Charles in Scotland, and won some incredible victories with his Highlanders, so that part of the Scottish army had to return home from England in order to fight him. The Royalist army in Cornwall was successful.

What really turned the tide for Parliament was the way it reorganized its army. There was a quarrel among its leaders. Oliver Cromwell accused the generals of being afraid to defeat the King outright. The Earl of Manchester said: 'If we beat the King ninety and nine times yet he is King still, and so will his *posterity* be after him, but if the King beats us then we shall all be hanged.' 'If this be so, my Lord,' retorted Oliver Cromwell, 'why did we take up arms at first?' The result of the angry debates in November and December 1644 was that all Members of Parliament were asked to resign from the army. This is known as the Self Denying Ordinance, and it was meant to be a tactful way of getting rid of the Earl of Essex and the Earl of Manchester. Sir Thomas Fairfax, who had fought well in Yorkshire, was made Commander-in-Chief. Oliver Cromwell, however, was reappointed to the army although he remained an M.P., and he became the General of the Cavalry. What was much more important was that there was only to be one army, under one commander, and not several different armies in different parts of the country. In each county controlled by Parliament, committees were set up to look after local defence and recruiting, and special weekly taxes had to be paid to support this new Army. The foot soldiers were paid 8*d* a day and out of this they had to pay for their food and clothing. The troopers got 2*s* a day for themselves and their horses. So long as they were paid regularly, this was a good wage and they were contented. All these changes meant that there was a 'New Model Army', properly trained, which was ready to fight anywhere for Parliament. Above all, it was commanded by men who were absolutely determined to defeat the King.

On 14 June 1645, the King's army met this New Model Army in the greatest battle of the Civil War at Naseby in Northamptonshire. The Royalists were completely outnumbered and defeated. The King barely escaped with his life. He tried to lead a last charge, but a Scottish lord near him, Lord Carnworth, seized the bridle of the King's horse and turned it away as he shouted, 'Will you go to your death?' It was a crushing defeat. Thousands of the King's men were killed or taken prisoner: almost all the officers were lost, all the ammunition and guns captured, and the King's personal possessions, including his letters, were captured with the coaches and wagons.

From then on, it became one long story of defeat for the King's supporters. The last battle was a small one near Stow-on-the-Wold in the Cotswolds in March 1646. There, Sir Jacob Astley, fighting in the last battle as he had done in the first one at Edgehill, is again remembered for what he said as he surrendered: 'You have done your work now and may go play, unless you fall out among yourselves.'

As the news came in of Parliament's victories, of Montrose at last defeated in Scotland, of towns and castles surrendering—Leicester, Bridgwater, Pontefract, Scarborough, Sherborne, Bristol, Chester—the King had to admit that he was defeated and that there was no hope left. Late in April, he slipped away secretly from Oxford, giving the town permission to submit after he had gone. He decided to surrender to the Scots rather than to Parliament, and he did so at Newark on 5 May 1646. The Scots took him as a prisoner to Newcastle, and then finding that he would not agree to any of the terms they offered him, they handed him over to Parliament.

By that time, Sir Jacob Astley's words to his victors were beginning to come true: they *were* quarrelling among themselves. Parliament ordered its army to disband now that the war was over, but the troops refused to do so. There was eighteen weeks' pay owing to the foot soldiers and forty-three weeks' pay owing to the cavalry, but Parliament offered them only six weeks' pay. The troops also protested against many of the Parliament's decisions, especially over religion. Many of them did not want to have Presbyterianism forced on them, for they belonged to other Puritan groups, most especially to the Independent group. The troops were very near mutiny, and they elected representatives, known as Agitators, to be their spokesmen in opposing Parliament.

Then, and no one really knows who was behind this idea, about 500 troops under a young officer called Cornet Joyce, rode to Holmby House, near Northampton, where the King was being held by Parliament, and asked him to go with them. Charles asked Joyce for his authority to do this, and Joyce simply pointed to his troops. The King smiled and said: 'It is as fair a commission, and as well written as I have ever seen a commission in my life—a company of handsome proper gentlemen.'

All this suited Charles very well. His only hope was that his enemies would quarrel among themselves. He played one side off against the other. Before the Army captured him, he had pretended to consider Parliament's offer that they should control the Army for a number of years and that there should be a trial period of Presbyterianism in England. Then he pretended to consider the various offers the Army made to him: that there should be religious toleration but that a Parliament should have

strong control over what he could do as King. Some of the officers knew very well that Charles was only playing with them. 'Sire,' said Henry Ireton, who was Cromwell's son-in-law, 'you have the intention to be the *arbitrator* between Parliament and us, and we mean it to be between your Majesty and Parliament.'

In fact, the King was secretly planning to escape and to begin fighting again.

Henry Ireton

On 11 November 1647, he escaped from Hampton Court, where he was then negotiating with both sides, and made for Carisbrooke Castle in the Isle of Wight. He thought that the Governor was a friend who would protect him, but instead Colonel Hammond held him there as a prisoner still, so that the King himself could not take any part in the Second Civil War although he had deliberately provoked it. Many areas rose again for the King. There were Royalist armies once more in Essex, Kent and Wales: the King's standard waved again over castles like Pontefract and Scarborough. A Scottish army, but this time a Royalist one, invaded

England. Fairfax defeated the Royalists in Kent and then in Essex. Cromwell took an army to Wales, put down the rising there, and then went north to defeat the Scots at Preston. By September 1648 it was all over. Those who had risen for the King in this second outbreak of Civil War were harshly treated, and some of the Royalists who had held Colchester for the King were executed.

Charles I had been completely defeated: the Roundheads had beaten the Cavaliers.

7

Going to War

If you had been a boy in 1642 when the war started, you would not necessarily have joined one of the armies, for everyone did not fight in the Civil War. The chances are, however, that you would have been affected by the war at some time or another.

If you were comfortably off and the son of a gentleman, you would probably have heard your father discussing the debates in Parliament in the years before, and you would already have begun to know what the war was about and whether you agreed with King or Parliament. So, once the war started, you would know which side you wanted to win and which army you would join if you decided to fight. If you were just an ordinary boy, perhaps working in the country, you might well have gone with your master to fight on whichever side he chose. Some ordinary working boys, however, deliberately chose which side they wished to fight for: many of the apprentices in London chose to fight for Parliament. But it is equally true that you might have been forced to join the troops in your district as a *pressed man*, whether you wanted to or not, to fight for the side which happened to be strongest around your home. Or if you did not join an army you might have to fight when the war came near your home, perhaps to defend your town during a siege.

When war broke out, those men who decided to fight from the beginning took down the armour which had been hanging on the walls of their houses for many years. There had been no fighting in England for so long that often when they came to try on the armour, it would not fit them. It had probably been made for their great-great-grandfathers. When Sir Edmund Verney got ready to go to Scotland with the King in 1639, he was in a great panic when he found that the helmet which he had at Claydon would not fit him, and the blacksmith had to make him a new one.

Once fighting began, however, men soon found that a full suit of armour was far too heavy and too hot to wear. A few wore full armour at first: the troop of cavalry led by Sir Arthur Haslerig in Parliament's army were nick-named 'the lobsters' because they did. Soon, most men only put their armour on when they had their pictures painted, as though it was their best dress. You will see that Sir Edmund Verney on p. 3 and Colonel Hutchinson on p. 6 wore their armour when they had their portraits painted, but we know that John Hutchinson did not wear any armour at all when he was fighting. His wife wrote that 'he put off a very good suit of armour that he had, which, being musket proof, was so heavy that it heated him, and so could not be persuaded to wear anything but a buff coat'.

Most men seem to have ended by wearing a buff coat when they were fighting. Buff is ox-hide treated with oil. It was made into a short coat which was fairly close fitting, with a slit at the back and sometimes with slits at the side, too. It had no sleeves or collar, so that the lace collar and the sleeves of the shirt underneath could be seen. You can see this sort of leather jerkin in the picture on page 76 of Charles I dictating a letter to his secretary Sir Edward

75

Charles I dictating a letter

Walker. The King is wearing a breastplate over his buff coat, but Sir Edward, who is using a drum as his writing-table, is wearing his coat without any armour over it. Most cavalry soldiers seem to have managed something half-way between full armour and Colonel Hutchinson's refusal to wear any. Over their buff coat they wore a breast-plate and a back-plate, with perhaps smaller pieces of steel called *tassets* to guard their thighs when fighting. Cavalry men also wore leather jack boots to protect their legs. Most men, though again not every one, wore a helmet which they always called a pot.

Foot soldiers wore their ordinary clothes: breeches, full length stockings pulled over the legs of their breeches, a coat and shoes. At first, they wore clothes of any colour—probably just the clothes they happened to be wearing when they joined—but soon all the men in one company began to wear coats of the same colour: red, blue, green, yellow, as their colonel or the county committee which had formed them chose. This was partly to help them to recognize each other in battle, but partly because it was easier and cheaper to buy a large amount of the same coloured material to make new coats. John Hampden dressed in green the men of Buckinghamshire who joined him to fight for Parliament. The Earl of Newcastle bought white undyed cloth for the men who joined him to fight for the King,

Riding boot

and they said that they would dye it red in the blood of their enemies. They became known as Newcastle's Whitecoats, but when at the battle of Marston Moor in 1644 they were completely outnumbered and fought on till only thirty of a thousand men were left alive, it was their own blood which dyed Newcastle's Whitecoats red. It was only when the New Model Army was formed for Parliament in 1645 that there was anything like a real uniform for a whole army. The men who had fought with Cromwell from the Eastern Association of the counties of East Anglia had always dressed in red coats. This colour was then chosen as the colour for all the men in the new Parliamentary army, and they were soon known as 'redcoats'.

When war began, however, because there was no uniform for either army, it was difficult to pick out friend from foe in the excitement of a battle. Even when regiments started to wear coats of the one colour, it still was not

77

easy to identify the two sides in a battle, for the same colours were used in both armies. The men therefore had secret signs, given out just before a battle began. At the battle of Marston Moor, for example, the Roundheads put a piece of white paper in their hats. When Sir Thomas Fairfax found himself cut off from his own men, he simply took the piece of white paper out of his hat, passed through the Royalists as though he was one of them, and made his way round to join Cromwell's cavalry on the other wing of the Parliamentary army. (Here is another reminder that you could not really tell Cavalier from Roundhead.) These field signs, as they were called, had to be something which could be chosen quickly and at the last possible moment before the battle began, so that the other side could not know the field sign for the day. At the battle of Naseby, the King's forces picked beanstalks and wore those as their field sign for the battle. There were also field words, or passwords, to help the men to recognize their own side during the fighting. At Naseby, the field word for the King's army was 'Queen Mary' while the Parliamentary army had 'God our strength' for theirs.

Once a battle had begun, it was difficult to give orders or instructions, and so there was a series of orders by bugles. Each company had its own flag or standard to help the men to keep together. The usual battle formation was to have the foot soldiers—*pikemen* and *musketeers*—in the centre. The cavalry were on either side of the foot soldiers as the right wing and the left wing of the armies.

The pikemen were always very tall strong men. They had to be because their pike was sixteen feet long: few of you will be in a classroom as high as that. At first, the pikemen wore helmets, breast- and back-plates and tassets but they soon stopped wearing armour, for they found that carrying the long pike with its heavy iron head, and their kit, was just about as much as they could manage without being burdened by armour. It was their task to stand firm in defence, with their long pikes levelled out preventing the enemy from piercing their lines; in attack, they went forward to push the other side back with 'push of pike'.

The musketeers could kill at a distance in a way that the pikemen could not, but firing a musket was a very slow job, and the musketeers might only be able to fire one volley before it became hand-to-hand fighting. Round his neck, a musketeer wore a wide leather band called a *bandolier* from which hung twelve leather or metal containers, each of which carried a charge of powder. Also slung round him somewhere was a flask with spare powder, a leather bag filled with lead bullets which weighed about an ounce each, and all the material which he needed for lighting and firing the charge. He carried a length of match, which was cord boiled in vinegar. This had to be kept alight if there was any chance of action, and, of course, this was difficult in wet weather. At the beginning of the war, the musketeers also carried a crutch of wood to balance their heavy muskets on as they loaded them and prepared to fire. Later on in the war, muskets were made lighter so that the men could hold them without the support of a crutch.

Pikeman

79

Musketeer

When the musketeer was ready to fire, he put a charge of powder from one of the bags on his bandolier down the muzzle of his musket, then he put a lead bullet in (he usually had one or two from his bag ready in his mouth), then a length of burning match was fixed in the cock, then a pinch of fine powder was placed as a *primer* in the pan in which the *cock* snapped down as he pressed the trigger. After all that, his range was only between 200 and 400 yards, and once he had fired, he had to begin the performance all over again. When he had fired, he was supposed to drop to the back of his line, while the man behind him stepped forward to fire. One of the improvements in the New Model Army was that its musketeers fired on a new principle learned from Sweden, which let three lines of men fire at one time, one kneeling, one stooping and one standing upright. Very often, however, after the first volley had been fired, the musketeers had to take refuge behind the pikemen, or else they just went in for hand-to-hand fighting, using their muskets as clubs. It was forty years after the Civil War before bayonets were invented: once that happened, musketeers had a weapon to fight with when they had fired their muskets.

Musketeers had a difficult and dangerous job. Sometimes a line of them was put in front of the army before a battle to try to ward off the first charge: Prince Rupert did this at Marston Moor. This was known as the 'forlorn hope'. When choosing the lie of the land on which to fight a battle, the generals had also to think about the direction of the wind, for it was hard for an army to fight if the smoke from the muskets drifted across their faces. At Naseby, the Royalists took up an unexpected position because of this. Keeping the match alight all the time was difficult, too, and at night it showed the enemy where you were. At times, however, the lighted match was an advantage. When the Parliamentarians wanted to slip away in the night after the battle of Lansdown in Somerset they hung lighted match over the walls and hedges to make it look to the Royalist sentries as though they were still there—and then they marched quietly away.

It was the cavalry, however, which decided battle after battle in the war. At first, the King had the better cavalry. His nephew, Prince Rupert, had learned a new way to use cavalry in the wars he had fought in Germany before he came to England to help his uncle. This was to attack the enemy swiftly in a terrific charge, using the weight and speed of the charge to break through the enemy lines, before firing any shots at all. Prince Rupert used this method at the first battle of Edgehill, instead of the older way of trotting up to the enemy, firing pistols, and then returning to your own lines to re-form, which was what the

Parliamentary cavalry did. Rupert's men charged right down the hill, and shattered Lord Essex's cavalry waiting to move slowly against them. The difficulty of this new way of fighting was to stop the galloping horsemen once they had broken through the enemy lines, and to get them back to the battlefield in good order to continue fighting. Prince Rupert was a magnificent fighter, but this was something he never learned to do. His victorious charge at Edgehill carried his cavalry on for miles, chasing and looting their defeated opponents. When Rupert returned to the field, it was to find the rest of the King's army hard pressed, and what might have been a victory for the King had been lost because the cavalry had not returned in time.

It was Oliver Cromwell who profited from Prince Rupert's mistakes. He had had no experience of war before Edgehill, but he watched Rupert's tactics closely, saw how to improve them, and taught his cavalry to keep together and to return quickly to the field. The result was that at Marston Moor, and at many other battles, it was the cavalry trained by Cromwell which was successful. Rupert nicknamed them 'Ironsides', not because they wore any other armour than the usual breast- and back-plates, tassets and 'pot', but because they kept so firmly together. At the battle of Naseby which finally decided the Civil War, it was the same story. Rupert kept his cavalry together better in that battle, but even so, by the time he got them back to the field, there was no work for them to do but to protect the King and the survivors as they fled from the battlefield.

Guns did not play very much part in the battles of the Civil War. They took so long to fire that if they were used, they could probably fire only one shot, and then the gunners had to retreat to the rear. Whoever won the battle won all the guns, too, as the Parliamentarians did at Naseby. The guns ranged from the demi-culverin which could fire a ball of nine to twelve pounds, to the drake which could fire a ball of three pounds. Most guns could only fire about fifteen shots an hour, and were dangerous to use. Their chief use was in sieges, either of towns or castles or houses, when they could be used to batter the walls down so that the attackers could try to enter through the *breach*.

Neither side wanted to keep prisoners, for they had no way of looking after them. Men taken prisoners were usually kept in the nearest church or castle, and as soon as possible they were exchanged for prisoners on the other side. Ralph Verney, as a Parliamentary supporter, spoke for his sister's Royalist husband when he was captured by Parliament and arranged an exchange for him. When Henry Verney was captured at Portsmouth, Ralph had some trouble in arranging to get his brother released, for Henry had fought so bravely for the King that the Parliamentary army wanted a good man of their own side back from the Royalists in return for Henry. Sometimes prisoners were put on their honour that they would not fight again and were then released to go back home. There was a man like that at Nottingham: a Royalist who had been captured by Colonel Hutchinson's men and had been put on his honour not to fight again. When the Royalist forces were besieging Nottingham Castle at one time, it would have been easy for this man to have taken the chance to break his word and join his own side again. When John Hutchinson was saved by the relieving Parliamentary forces, he was so pleased that the Cavalier had kept his word that he freed him from his promise and sent him away.

Prisoners often joined the side which had captured

them. There were many men on both sides who did not really mind which side they fought on. Many did not want to fight far away from their own homes. Even the troops from London who were among the best in the Parliamentary army were said to cry 'Home, home' if they had been away for more than a few weeks. Both armies had many men deserting throughout the war because of this.

For both sides, the problem was how to pay for their armies. The King's wealthy supporters like the Earl of Newcastle and the Marquis of Worcester gave their lands and money to him and the Oxford colleges melted down their gold and silver plate for the King. Parliament was better able to tax the areas it controlled, and county committees raised money for forces. In both armies, however, pay was usually behindhand. Lucy Hutchinson wrote that when her husband was governor of Nottingham Castle for Parliament during the war, 'the poor soldiers had such short pay that they were, for the most part, thirty weeks and more behind; and when they marched out at any time, the governor would not suffer them to take a cup of drink unpaid for in the country but always, whenever they took refreshment in their marches, paid for it himself'. John Hutchinson was an exception in trying to pay for what his men needed. On both sides, soldiers could often only get food and drink by looting and plundering. In the end, there were whole districts where the farmers and ordinary people banded themselves into groups known as Clubmen, ready to fight the men of either armies when they came near in search of food or horses.

Although the soldiers of the Civil War and the way they fought seem very far removed from soldiers and warfare today, yet there are direct links between them and the modern British Army. The Grenadier Guards trace their descent back to the troop raised in 1656 by Charles II among the royalist exiles in the Netherlands, and they returned with him at the Restoration. The Coldstream Guards come from the troops raised by General Monk, who came down with him from Scotland to put an end to the confusion in England after Cromwell's death and called the Parliament which brought back Charles II. The Life Guards were raised in 1660 from Royalist followers of Charles II at the time of the Restoration. When, today, the Guards are in full dress on a state occasion like Trooping the Colour or on duty at Buckingham Palace, they still wear the colour of the New Model Army which defeated Charles I. Red was the colour of the British uniform from the days of the redcoats of the Roundhead army until the early years of this century. It was then decided that it was more sensible to wear khaki when fighting, so red is now only worn on ceremonial occasions.

8

Women and Girls in the Time of the Civil War

What was happening to the women and girls while their husbands and brothers were fighting for King or Parliament? Did they live their ordinary lives or did they get caught up in the war itself and do brave deeds? These were out-of-the-ordinary days and yet ordinary life had to go on. So, first, we shall find out about the way they lived when life was peaceful: then we shall see what happened to some women when war came their way.

If you had been a girl then, would you have gone to school or had lessons? The answer seems to be that some girls did, and some did not. It all depended on what your parents wanted. It does not seem to have been necessary to belong to a wealthy family, as Lucy Hutchinson did, so that your parents could afford to pay for teachers for you if they wished you to be educated. Some of the maids who worked for the Verney family at Claydon could read and write, so there must sometimes have been a village school, or someone who taught poorer girls, too, if their parents wanted it.

Lucy Hutchinson wrote of herself that 'by the time I was four years old, I could read English perfectly. When I was about seven years old, I had at one time eight tutors in languages, music, dancing and needlework. My father would have me learn Latin, and I was so apt that I outstripped my brothers who were at school'. She said that she loved reading and learning, but 'as for music, I profited very little in them and would never practice my lute or harpsichord but when my masters were with me, and as for my needle, I absolutely hated it'. Lucy was evidently an exceptional girl with unusual parents, but one of Ralph's cousins, Nan Denton, sounds equally clever and she had a father who was keen that she should be taught well. Nan wrote to Ralph to say that she was going to learn Latin, Greek and Hebrew and that her father approved of this. Ralph, however, did not. He replied: 'believe me, a Bible (with the Book of Common Prayer) and a good catechism in your mother tongue, is worth all the rest and much more suitable to your sex. I know your father thinks this is false doctrine, but be confident that your husband will be of my opinion.' (If Nan's future husband when she grew up was going to be anyone like John Hutchinson, he would not agree with Ralph, for John fell in love with Lucy and married her just because

Children playing

87

she was so clever.) Ralph loved his own daughter, Peg, very much but by the time she was eight, Peg had only been taught some music and embroidery. Evidently Ralph did not believe in education for girls and he said that he thought Peg was 'very backward' but she would be 'scholar enough for a woman'. He agreed that Nan ought to learn French, but only so that she could then read the 'receipts for preserving, making creams, and all sorts of cookery, ordering your garden, and in brief, all manners of good housewifery'.

So many of the diaries and accounts of the Civil War period were written by women that it is clear that at least the better-off girls learned to read and write, but for most girls their main education was learning to be good house-wives from their mothers. Women, even those who were rich and had lots of servants, worked hard in their homes. So many things were made at home which today we buy: it was indeed a full-time job to run a home. Women had to know how to make almost everything needed in a home, including medicines. Lady Verney, Sir Edmund Verney's wife made all her own linen sheets for the household; they were spun and woven at Claydon. When Sir Thomas Gardiner, an old friend of the Verneys, wrote to Sir Edmund one day, he apologized for the fact that his wife was too busy to add a message to his letter, she 'being almost melted with the double heat of the weather and her em-ployment, because the fruit is suddenly ripe and she is so busy preserving'. Lady Gardiner had almost thirty ser-vants, but she still made the jam herself. Ralph's wife, Mary, was very good at baking bread: after she had been staying with Ralph's uncle in London, he said that he would miss her company, but that he would also miss her to 'roast my apples, and provide me with bread and saus-ages and make *pottage*'.

Marriages were almost always arranged by the parents. It was a business arrangement, in which the income which the young couple would have was quite openly discussed between the two families. It was only when the money matters had been settled, and it had been agreed between the two sets of parents that the young couple would have enough to live on, that the two young people were allowed to meet. Even so, the young man and woman seem to have had a fair amount of choice. They were not forced to marry each other, if one did not like the other once they had met, even if all the money arrangements had been made to the parents' satisfaction. Most marriages we know of were arranged like this, and most seem to have been very happy. Sir Edmund and Lady Verney's marriage had been settled in this way, but they were devoted to each other. Sir Edmund used to begin his letters to his wife 'Dear Puss', and they sound like the letters of a very happily married couple. The marriage of their son, Ralph, to Mary Blacknall was even more complicated than the usual arranged marriage.

Mary Blacknall was left an orphan at the age of nine, when her parents died of the plague. She then came under the Court of Wards, which was one of Charles I's ways of making money. A group of her relations had to pay the King £1,000, and promise to pay another £1,000 later, in order to get the right to be her guardians and to hold her lands for her. One uncle tried to marry her to his son in order to get possession of her money, but the others stopped him from doing this. Eventually, the other guardians offered her to Sir Edmund Verney for his son Ralph. Sir Edmund paid Mary's relations £1,000 for this marriage, for her money would then belong to Ralph, but they still said that she should not be forced into the marriage if she did not like Ralph when they met. However, she

A ladies' party

did, and the young couple were married. Mary was
then thirteen, and Ralph was fifteen. They did not live
together for another two years, but continued to live in
their own homes. Then, when Ralph was eighteen and
still an undergraduate at Oxford, Mary went to live with
him and her father- and mother-in-law at Claydon. Yet
there could not have been a happier marriage, for Mary
and Ralph loved each other dearly. They had five children,
of whom only two lived. Ralph was brokenhearted when
Mary died at the age of thirty-three. He never married
again, unlike many of his friends, and he grieved for Mary
till he himself died many years later when he was eighty-
three years old. Sir Edmund and Lady Verney grew very
fond of their son's wife when Mary came to live with
them, and she got on very well with all her brothers- and
sisters-in-law and often kept the peace between them when
they quarrelled. Their favourite nickname for Mary was
'Mischief', but young Mun always called her 'my sweetest
sister'. So a marriage which had not a very promising be-

ginning, turned out very happily for Mary. Of all Ralph's sisters, the only one who made an unhappy marriage was Margaret, and yet she was the one who had most say in her own marriage, for an aunt had left her some money of her own.

John Hutchinson and Lucy Apsley fell in love with each other when they met: indeed, John had fallen in love with her before they met, for he had seen some of her Latin books in her home and heard a song for which she had written the words. He said 'I cannot be at rest till this lady's return that I may be acquainted with her.' Lucy was away at the time with her parents who were arranging a marriage for her which she would not accept. When they returned home, John Hutchinson met her and fell in love with her. His own father, however, was busy arranging a marriage for him, and John had to ask his father to release him from that marriage so that he could tell Lucy that he loved her. Then their parents agreed, and they were married. John was twenty-two and Lucy was eighteen: this was quite old by the standards of the day. Girls could be married at twelve and boys at fourteen, and they were often married at this age, although, like Ralph and Mary Verney, they went on living in their own homes for a few years before they began to live together.

When the Civil War began, many women had to face hardships and sorrow. Mary Verney herself had to become a poor refugee. Do you remember how Ralph, after first supporting Parliament, could not agree to take the Oath of the Solemn League and Covenant in 1643? This meant that Ralph and Mary had to leave their comfortable home at Claydon and go sadly across the Channel to live in poverty in France. Mary was a brave and clever woman, able to do all her husband's business in London, but she just could not dress herself! So, although they were

A kitchen maid

now so poor, they took two of their maids from Claydon with them to France. Bess did the cooking and housework, and Luce dressed her mistress and helped Bess a little. Luce and Bess soon learned to speak French better than either Ralph or Mary Verney. When Mary returned to England in 1646 to try to get a pardon for Ralph from Parliament, Luce came with her but decided that she wanted to stay in England and not live in France any more. This worried Ralph and Mary, for they felt that no other English maid would be prepared to share their hardships, and yet Mary must have someone to dress her. Ralph wrote to Mary when he heard the news that Luce did not want to come back: 'I know no English maid will ever be content (or stay a week) to fare as these servants fare . . . No English maids will be content with our diet or way of living.' He said that he had roast meat only once a week 'which were strange in an English maid's opinion'. Mary tried hard to find someone to take the place of Luce. Ralph wrote: 'You say chamber maids will have four or five pounds wages and neither wash nor starch: that is to say they will do nothing but dress you, for I do not value their needlework at a *groat* a month. Tis true if any of us should be sick you would want one to make such broths and such like matters' but he felt that although Luce could do this, perhaps other maids would not. In the end, their problem was settled because Luce decided to stay with them after all, while Bess said that she 'had no thoughts of parting, and that if we stayed half a dozen years abroad, we might assure ourselves of her'. Ralph was so pleased with Bess's loyalty to them that he gave her a pair of gloves as a present which cost him £1 5s 0d.

Ralph and Mary left a sad household behind at Claydon. Before he went into exile, Ralph tried to make arrangements for his sisters to be looked after, for he was the head of his family now that his father had been killed at the battle of Edgehill, and his brothers were still fighting for the King. There was his eldest sister, Susan, who was twenty-two years of age, and then there were Penelope, Peg, Molly, and Betty, the youngest, who was twelve years of age. Perhaps because they were so anxious and unhappy about big things, the sisters quarrelled among themselves about little things. They even quarrelled about which maid they would have to dress them, though they were now poor and would have to economize. Nan Fudd, who had been their nurse when they were all babies, still lived with them at Claydon and they loved her, and they liked Bess Coleman, another of the maids. Penelope wrote grumbling to Ralph: 'I am to intreat a favour, that is if you can let Nann fud have soe much time as to come my head for I doe heare that bess colman cannot doe it and if I have not won that can come a hed will, I doe not know what toe do by reason that my hed is so tender and to smoth sum of my upper lining.' (Like so many letters of this time, you will probably have to read this aloud to understand what Penelope was writing: she wants Nan Fudd to comb her hair, and by smoothing her linen she means to iron her clothes.) It seems strange that Mary and the girls made so much fuss about being unable to comb their own hair or to dress themselves, for the styles of the day do not look difficult ones. It would have been different if the girls had lived, say, in the eighteenth century when women had hooped dresses and wore high powdered hair styles. It is not as though they were helpless and inefficient in other ways.

Perhaps, as so often happens, it means that they grumbled about small things but could rise to the occasion when there was a crisis, for many of the women of the time were full of bravery and courage when it was needed. With their husbands away, either with the King or Parliament's forces, it was left to the women to run the farms or the businesses, to look after their houses, and perhaps to defend them.

This happened, for example, to Lady Bankes and her daughters at Corfe Castle in Dorset. When her husband sent her and the children there for safety, Lady Bankes got in stores of food in case their house was ever besieged, as finally it was in the spring of 1643. Lady Bankes made her house a stronghold for the King, and it was attacked by their friends and neighbours who supported Parliament. She was sent some soldiers from the Royalist army of the district to help her to defend the castle for the

Ruins of Corfe Castle today

94

King. She and her daughters joined the soldiers on the castle walls in flinging stones and hot coals down on the attackers who were climbing up by ladders. The siege was called off in the August, and Lady Bankes continued to hold Corfe Castle for the King almost till the end of the war. She was besieged again from 20 June 1645 until the end of February 1646, so her home was among the last to surrender to Parliament, and even then it was taken by treachery and not by direct assault. The walls of the castle were then destroyed to make sure that it could never be used again, but thanks to some of her friends and neighbours who had been in the attacking force, Lady Bankes was treated kindly. She had, however, like all other Cavalier families, to pay heavy fines for having fought against Parliament.

Charlotte, Countess of Derby

Charlotte, Countess of Derby, had a similar time at her home at Lathom House in Lancashire. Her husband was away with the King's forces when she was summoned to surrender her home by the Parliamentary Governor of Manchester. She refused, and was besieged by a Roundhead force from March until May 1644. She had a garrison of 300 soldiers to fight for her, but she helped to organize the defence and to look after the soldiers while her daughters stayed near her. One of the soldiers said that 'the little ladies had stomachs to digest the cannon'. They were rescued by Prince Rupert with his army on their way to the battle of Marston Moor. As a reward for her bravery in holding out for the King, Prince Rupert presented Lady Derby with twenty-two of the flags which 'three days before were proudly before her house'. Finally, when she was away from home with her husband on the Isle of Man, Lathom House was again besieged and this time it had to surrender. One of the Parliamentary newspapers, in reporting its capture, said that Lady Derby had shown herself to be 'the better soldier of the two' compared with her husband.

The Parliamentary ladies who defended their homes against Royalist forces were equally brave. Brilliana, Lady Harley, defended her home at Brampton in Herefordshire for six weeks until the Royalist troops were called away because they were needed elsewhere. We are told of one lady, Mrs Purefroy, who supported Parliament. She defended her home against Prince Rupert and 500 of his men although she had only her daughter and son-in-law, three maids and three menservants in the house with her. Between them, they had twelve muskets but they shot three captains and fifteen of Rupert's men before they had to surrender. Prince Rupert was so impressed by their bravery in holding out against such heavy odds that he would not let his soldiers plunder the house when the little garrison surrendered to him.

The usual fate of a house when it was surrendered was to be looted, and then it was often pulled down so that it could not be used again. Some of Ralph's cousins were left homeless in this way. First of all, their home was taken over by a hundred Parliamentary troops, so they were tightly packed in the house. Then the Roundheads went away, and the King's forces took the house over, dug a trench round it and placed guns there so that they could defend it against Parliament. Then the house was attacked by a cavalry troop under Oliver Cromwell and had to surrender to him. It was looted and burned to the ground. The women and children of the family were left to make their way across the fields to take refuge in Ralph's home at Claydon. 'We were not shamefully treated in any way by the soldiers,' wrote Pen Denton to Ralph, 'but they took everything and I was not left scarce the clothes on my back.'

Not only had women to learn to take events like this in their stride, but their good training in household matters stood them in good stead. Part of their training to be good housewives included knowing something about medicine and nursing, for when a doctor came, he stayed several days and was expensive, so he was sent for only in a real emergency. Lucy Hutchinson was only one of many women who could look after the sick and wounded as well as any doctor. When men were wounded in Nottingham Castle while her husband was holding the castle for Parliament, she said that 'she having some excellent plasters in her closet, with the aid of a gentleman that had some skill, dressed all their wounds, whereof some were dangerous being all shots, with such good success, that they were all cured in convenient time'. She insisted on nursing the wounded Royalist prisoners, too. One of her husband's Puritan officers told her that he disapproved of this, but she said 'she had done nothing but what she thought was her duty, in humanity to them, as fellow-creatures, not enemies'.

Naturally, we know more about the women who did outstanding things, but there must have been just as many ordinary women who were brave. For example, when Nottingham Castle had been besieged by the Royalist forces, and then rescued by Parliamentary forces, a great deal of damage had been done to the town in the fighting. Houses—they must have been the old timber houses—were left smouldering after the Royalist forces had tried to set them on fire. Colonel Hutchinson organized the women of Nottingham into parties of fifty, and they patrolled the town at nights to watch out for fires, and to prevent the Royalists from setting fire to any more.

There must, however, have been many women on both sides who were left with hearts as sad as Ralph Verney's cousin, Doll Leake. When she heard the news that Mun had been killed after the fall of Drogheda in 1649, she wrote 'I cannot express how unhappy I am,' and she said that now every one she knew who had fought in the Civil War had been killed.

9

The Trial of the King

The Army which had fought for Parliament was in an angry mood when the King began the Civil War for the second time. When he was defeated again in 1648, they resolved to take matters into their own hands and have 'Charles Stuart — that man of blood' punished, for they said that it was his fault that there had been Civil War. Colonel Pride and some soldiers stood at the entrance to Parliament one day in December 1648 to prevent any M.P. who did not agree with the Army from entering the House of Commons. They allowed only 46 M.P.s to take their seats. Even so, only 26 of these voted that the King should be brought to trial, and 20 voted against it. When the House of Lords would not agree to a trial, this handful of M.P.s in the Commons decided that they had complete authority to do it on their own. On 2 January 1649 they voted 'for the erection of a High Court of Justice for trying Charles Stuart, King of England'. They appointed 135 men to be the King's judges, men whom they felt sure would find the King guilty.

About two o'clock on the afternoon of Saturday, 20 January 1649, Charles I was brought into Westminster Hall to begin his trial under a guard of soldiers who wore the red uniform of the New Model Army. The King was dressed in black, with the blue ribbon of the Garter

The trial of Charles I (from a drawing made later)

around his neck, and he wore a tall black hat. He sat down without removing his hat to show that he did not respect this court.

You can still see the Hall today when you visit the Houses of Parliament, for although the House of Commons and the House of Lords had to be rebuilt after a great fire in 1834, the Hall escaped damage and survives as a link between the old Palace of Westminster and the present Houses of Parliament. In those days, the Hall was used as a market, but the tradesmen's stalls had been cleared away for the King's trial. At one end of the Hall, rows of benches had been built for the men who were to act as the King's judges. In front of them was a crimson velvet chair for Henry Bradshaw, who had been made the President of the Court. Facing these, a little distance away, was another red velvet chair for the prisoner. Down each side of the Hall, galleries had been erected for ladies and for others who had been especially invited. Then, after a space, a railing had been placed across the Hall to hold back the spectators who were later allowed to crowd in at the back to watch the trial.

Of the 135 men appointed to be judges, 50 refused to come to the Hall. Algernon Sydney had said to Oliver Cromwell: 'First, the King can be tried by no court; secondly, no man can be tried by this court,' and presumably many of the others who refused to come felt the same as he did. Oliver Cromwell and Henry Ireton were the only two important Army officers who were present. Among those who did not come was Lord Fairfax, the Commander-in-Chief of the Army which had defeated the King. As the judges' names were called out, there was no answer when it came to Lord Fairfax's name. Instead, a woman's voice from one of the galleries called, 'Not here, and never will be: he has too much sense.' It was his wife, Lady Fairfax, and she was hustled away. One of those who did accept the invitation to attend the trial as a judge was John Hutchinson. His wife said that it was 'very much against his will' that he was made a judge, 'but looking upon himself as called hereunto, durst not refuse it, as holding himself by the covenant of God and the public trust of his country reposed in him, although he was not ignorant of the danger he ran'.

The charge was read out, accusing Charles Stuart of being a 'tyrant, traitor, murderer and a public and *implacable* enemy to the commonwealth of England' and saying that by his 'cruel and unnatural wars by him, the said Charles Stuart, levied, continued and renewed, much innocent blood of the free people of this nation has been spilt'. We are told that the King laughed when the clerk read this out to the court. 'First I must know,' he said, 'by what power I am called hither before I will give answer.' He insisted that a man could only be tried by lawful judges and added 'Remember, I am your King, your lawful King, and what sins you bring upon your heads.' Bradshaw replied that the King was being tried by the 'authority of the Commons of England, assembled in Parliament on behalf of the people of England by which people you are elected King'.

Charles pointed out immediately that he was not an elected King. 'I deny that. England was never an elected kingdom. It was an *hereditary* kingdom for near this thousand years.' He claimed that 'I am entrusted with the liberty of my people. I do stand more for the liberties of my people than anyone that is seated here as a judge. Therefore show me by what lawful authority I am seated here and I will answer it. Otherwise I will not betray the liberties of my people.' Throughout the rest of the trial, Charles returned to this point again and again. As King, it was his duty to protect the liberties of his people. If any group that chose could set itself up as a court, and men could call themselves judges without any real authority other than their own wishes, then no one in England could be free.

The Court did not sit on the Sunday, but when it met again at nine o'clock on the Monday morning, the King repeated his refusal to recognize the Court. 'It is not my case alone. It is the freedom and liberty of the people of England. For if power without law may make law, may alter the *fundamental* laws of the kingdom, I do not know what subject in England can be assured of his life or anything he can call his own'. Bradshaw interrupted him to say that he must not discuss the authority of the Court and refused to allow the King to continue. The clerk was ordered to read the charge again that Charles Stuart was accused of high treason by the people of England, and the King was ordered to give 'a positive answer whether you confess or deny the charges'. Once more the King replied: 'I will answer the same as soon as I know by what authority you sit.' Bradshaw said: 'Sir, 'tis not for prisoners to require.' The King replied: 'Sir, I am not an ordinary prisoner.' Bradshaw shouted: 'Take away the prisoner,' and we are told that as the guards led the King out of the Hall the crowds behind the barrier shouted 'God save the King'.

Much the same sort of thing happened on Tuesday, the third day of the trial. Charles said: 'It is for the liberties of the people of England that I stand for. For me to acknowledge a new Court I never heard of before—I, that am your King, that should be an example to all the people of England to uphold justice, to maintain the old laws—indeed I do not know how to do it.' Once more he refused to reply to the charge that Charles Stuart had been accused of 'high crimes and treasons' against the people of England. Bradshaw said: 'This is the third time that you have publicly disowned this Court. How far you have preserved the fundamental laws and freedom of the subject, your own actions have spoken it.' He said that the King had written his actions in the blood which had been shed through the war, and he ordered the guards to take the King away.

For the next three days, Cromwell and some of the judges met in secret to decide what to do. By this time there were only about 60 men prepared to go on sitting as judges of the King. It was decided to sentence the King to death without any further trial on the Saturday, and Cromwell and some of the others began to sign the death warrant on the Friday. John Hutchinson was one of those who remained as a judge to the end. He felt that the

King must be punished for all the 'blood and desolation' which he had brought to the country through the war and which would happen again if they let him escape. His wife, Lucy, wrote: 'As for Mr Hutchinson, although he was very much confirmed in his judgement concerning the case, yet herein being called to an extraordinary action, whereof many were of several minds (she means that they were of differing opinions), he addressed himself to God by prayer; desiring the Lord that, if through any human *frailty* he were led into any error or false opinion in these great transactions he would open his eyes, and not suffer him to proceed.' After praying for guidance, and after discussing it with 'conscientious, upright and *unbiased* persons,' John Hutchinson 'signed the sentence against the king.'

Then the court met again on the Saturday. Bradshaw had begun to say that all knew that the prisoner had been brought before them three times to answer to the charges of treason in the name of the people of England, when a voice called out: 'Not half or a quarter of them. Oliver Cromwell is a traitor.' It was a woman in one of the galleries, wearing a mask—and almost certainly Lady Fairfax again. She had to be removed from the Hall before Bradshaw went on to say that as the prisoner refused to plead, sentence would be passed on him. The King asked if he could be allowed to speak to the House of Lords and the House of Commons, but Bradshaw said that this was just another attack on the court. Then there was another interruption as one of the judges, Colonel Downes, asked that the King should be allowed to do this. Obviously, Colonel Downes must have had a last minute panic about what was happening, but Cromwell sent him away so that the court could continue. Sentence was then passed on the King. He had been found guilty of levying war against his Parliament and people, and was therefore guilty of high treason. 'For all which treasons and crimes, this Court doth adjudge that the said Charles Stuart, as a tyrant, traitor, murderer and public enemy to the good of this nation, shall be put to death by severing of his head from his body.' The King tried to speak, but he was not allowed to do so, and as the guards led him away, he was heard to say: 'Expect what justice other people will have.'

On the Sunday, the King was moved from the Palace of Whitehall, where he had stayed during his trial, so that he would not hear the noise of the carpenters building the scaffolding outside the Banqueting Hall. Two of his children were still in England, and they were brought to him in his new rooms at St James's Palace to say goodbye to him. Elizabeth, who was thirteen years of age, was in tears, and her little brother Henry, who was ten, began to cry with her. The King took them on his knees and comforted them. He told them to love their mother, and made them both promise that they would look on their eldest brother Charles as King once their father was dead. Their brother Charles was in exile with the Queen and the other children, and the King was afraid that Parliament might take the chance of having Henry as their prisoner to make him into the sort of King they wanted. Charles I made little Henry promise that he would never let this happen. Then he gave the children the few jewels he had left with him, kissed them, blessed them, and had to let them go.

It was a bitterly cold day on Tuesday, 30 January 1649. The King put on an extra shirt in case he should shiver with cold and that might make people think that he was afraid. Then he put on a black satin doublet and breeches, though he said it was 'not in mourning', a red silk striped waistcoat, and the blue ribbon of the Garter. Over this, he put on a short black velvet cloak. He had his hair and beard, now going grey, trimmed carefully so that he would look neat. By eight o'clock he was ready, and Bishop Juxon came to stay with him till the end.

At ten o'clock the guards came to take the King to Whitehall. There, as he waited for the summons to go to his execution, he prayed with Bishop Juxon. Five Puritan ministers were sent by the judges who had signed his death warrant but the King said 'They, that have so often and ceaselessly prayed against me, shall never pray with me in this agony. They may, if they please, and I'll thank them for it, pray for me.' Dinner was prepared for the King, but he would not have anything for he wished to eat nothing between Holy Communion and his death. At last, Bishop Juxon persuaded him to have something in case he fainted on the scaffold because it was so cold, and Charles then ate a little bread and had a glass of wine. It was two o'clock in the afternoon before he was sent for. The delay had been because no one could be found who was willing to execute the King. The public hangman is said to have refused to do it, and to this day, we do not really know who were the two headsmen on the scaffold. They wore masks and false beards to disguise themselves.

The King was led to the Banqueting Hall of the Palace, the hall which he had had built and which Rubens had painted. It had been the scene of many of his happiest and gayest memories of life at Court before the war. It is the only part of the Palace of Whitehall which now survives, but we do not know which of the windows you can see today was the one from which the King stepped on to the scaffold.

There were black cloths hung from the railings of the scaffold, so no one standing in Whitehall could see the

The Banqueting Hall of Whitehall Palace

block. There were so many soldiers on guard that the spectators were too far away to hear what the King said, and only the fifteen people on the scaffold itself were able to hear his speech. He began by insisting on his innocence 'for all the world knows that I never did begin a war with the two Houses of Parliament. And I call God to witness, to whom I must shortly make an account, that I never did intend for to *encroach* on their privileges. They began on me . . . they began these unhappy troubles, not I.' As he talked about this, he showed that the memory of Strafford's death still haunted him: 'I will only say that an unjust sentence that I suffered for to take effect is punished now by an unjust sentence on me.' 'For the people,' he continued, 'truly I desire their liberty and freedom as much as anybody whomsoever. But I must tell you their liberty and freedom consists in having of government; those laws by which their life and goods may be most their own. It is not for having a share in government. That is nothing *pertaining to* them.' So, although Charles I was right when he had pleaded at his trial that there can be no freedom when there are unjust courts, yet to the end he held to his theory of the rights and duty of a king: it was for a king to

Charles I's speech on the scaffold (from a drawing made afterwards)

decide what was good for his people, not the people themselves. The Civil War had not changed his views. Because
he believed that this was the best way for subjects to be
happy, he said on the scaffold: 'I am the martyr of the
people.' Bishop Juxon reminded him that there was something more he wished to say, and then Charles declared:
'I die a Christian according to the profession of the Church
of England.' He told the executioner: 'I shall say but very
short prayers, and when I thrust out my hands . . .'

The crowd could only see the axe as it flashed down:
there was a loud groan from them as it did so. Afterwards
people paid to go up to see the scaffold, and the soldiers

sold pieces of wood on which the blood had splashed and handfuls of the sawdust which had been put down to soak it up. The King's body was put into a plain coffin, and four of his most faithful friends were allowed to stay with it all that night in the Banqueting Hall. They were the Duke of Richmond, the Earl of Hertford, the Earl of Lindsay and the Earl of Southampton. All four of them had asked to be allowed to die instead of the King. While Lord Southampton was taking his turn to be with the coffin during the night, a man, heavily muffled in a cloak, came into the Hall. He stood by the coffin for some time, and as he went away as quietly as he had come, he sighed and said 'Cruel necessity'. Lord Southampton could not be sure, but he thought it was Oliver Cromwell. Later, the four lords went with the coffin to Windsor Castle and buried the King in St George's Chapel there.

Protests against the trial of the King came from all over the country, from Scotland and from abroad. On the very morning of the King's execution, special Ambassadors from the Netherlands appealed to the House of Commons to spare the King's life. After the execution, the post was stopped for several weeks to try to prevent the news from spreading. Ralph Verney, by then living at Blois in France, got the news from an English merchant who lived in Rouen and who presumably got the news from sailors. Mr Cockram wrote from Rouen to send Ralph 'the doleful news of our King's death who was beheaded last Tuesday was seven night, at two o'clock, before Whitehall, the most barbarous act and lamentable sight that ever any Christians did behold . . . that woeful end, which makes all honest hearts to bleed, and is a beginning of England's greater miseries than ever hath been hitherto'. So shocked were French people at the news that another of Ralph's friends living in France had to ask Ralph not to put the word 'English' on the reply. He said in a postscript to his own letter: 'Pray, sir, write not the superscription "anglais" for that nation is so much in hatred that he cannot pass in the streets for safety.' Sir Roger Burgoyne, who was a staunch Parliamentarian, nevertheless wrote to Ralph: 'I would be content to be a monk or a hermit rather than a statesman in the present conjunction of affairs. . . . What will become of us in England, God only knows.' When Ralph's uncle, Dr Denton, was at last able to write again from London, he said: 'It is feared that the sword will govern instead of the crown.'

The Great Seal

10

Without a King

For the next nine years Oliver Cromwell, backed by the army, was the ruler of England and Wales, Scotland and Ireland: the sword governed instead of the crown, as Dr Denton had feared. Yet Cromwell did not want this to happen and made many attempts to find a different way of ruling. But it always came back to the fact that he was the only man strong enough to rule, and that he could only rule with the help of the army.

His story is an amazing one. He was a country gentleman from Huntingdonshire, where he lived for many years without being famous at all. He was elected an M.P. in 1628 and again for the Short Parliament and the Long Parliament in 1640. When the Long Parliament began, Sir Phillip Warwick described him as wearing 'a plain cloth suit which seemed to have been made by an ill country tailor: his linen was plain and not very clean: and I remember a speck or two of blood upon his little band, which was not much larger than his collar: his hat was without a hat band: his *stature* was of a good size, his sword stuck close to his side, his countenance swollen and reddish, his voice sharp and untuneable, and his *eloquence* full of fervour'.

Cromwell spoke mostly in the debates on religion, for he was against all that Charles and Archbishop Laud wanted

Oliver Cromwell

for the Church. He himself was an Independent—what we should now call a Congregationalist—and he believed that everyone should worship God in his own way. Once, when he was speaking in a debate, Lord Digby asked another M.P. who the 'slovenly fellow' was. The man he asked was John Hampden, Cromwell's cousin, who said: 'That slovenly fellow, I say that sloven, if we should come to a breach with the King (which God forbid) will be one of the greatest men of England.'

When it came to the 'breach with the King', Cromwell gathered about sixty men from his own district to fight for Parliament. They were all farmers and used to horses, but they needed training. When Cromwell saw at the first battle of Edgehill how successful the King's cavalry was, he went back home and set to work to train a troop of cavalry men who became the greatest fighters for Parliament. Cromwell's success in the war was partly because his men trusted and obeyed him completely and also because he chose his men carefully. He wanted a man 'who knows what he is fighting for and loves what he knows'. It was chiefly thanks to him and his cavalry that the New Model Army defeated the King in the last great battle of the Civil War at Naseby in 1645.

After the defeat of the King, Cromwell was in a difficult position. He had hoped that, after the war, there might be freedom for the men who believed, as he did, that there was no need for everyone to belong to the one Church. Parliament, however, insisted on Presbyterianism as the only religion in England. Cromwell agreed with those soldiers in the Army who opposed Parliament by asking for religious freedom, but he disagreed with other soldiers who also wanted the right to vote. These men were influenced by a writer called John Lilburne who taught that every freeborn Englishman (except servants, labourers and those who had fought for the King) should be able to vote in elections. Lilburne's followers were called Levellers because they believed that all men should be on the same level. Cromwell, however, thought that only people who owned houses and land were fit to have the vote. Because he was an M.P. as well as a general, he tried to keep Parliament and the Army together, but in the end he decided to side with the Army rather than with Parliament, whatever difficulties the Levellers might make for him.

Then he had to face a mutiny. The Levellers believed that the Grandees (the senior officers) were betraying them, so nine regiments mutinied. Cromwell and Fairfax went to meet them. The Leveller soldiers had papers in their hats with 'England's Freedom! Soldiers' Rights!' printed on them. When Fairfax spoke to the soldiers, eight regiments took the papers out of their hats, but one regiment refused. Cromwell charged into the men with

113

his sword drawn and the soldiers, who still respected him, scattered before him. They then surrendered and asked for mercy. The ringleaders were arrested and three of them condemned to death for mutiny. Cromwell then offered the three men the chance to draw lots, so that only one of them was shot for leading the mutiny. After this Fairfax and Cromwell were masters of the Army.

After the execution of the King, Cromwell's great problem was how to find a new way of governing the country. The House of Commons had shrunk to less than a hundred M.P.s: that was all that was left of the 552 who had been elected to the Long Parliament in 1640. All who had fought for the King and all those, like Ralph Verney, who had not agreed with Parliament during the war, were excluded. What was left was nicknamed 'the Rump', because it was only the tail of a Parliament. The Rump abolished the House of Lords and set up a Council of State of forty members, with Oliver Cromwell as chairman. England was declared to be a Commonwealth.

But people could not agree on how the country should be governed. The Levellers, in particular, grumbled against the new government. John Lilburne soon found himself imprisoned and then banished. Cromwell stamped out mutinies among Levellers in the Army. 'I tell you,' he said to the Council of State, 'you have no other way to deal with these men but to break them, or they will break you.'

Cromwell had problems outside England as well. First he had to go to Ireland to fight the Royalists there. One of these was young Mun Verney. He had escaped to Ireland after the King's defeat and was now fighting for the Royalists there. He was killed after Cromwell captured a town called Drogheda with great cruelty. When Cromwell had conquered in Ireland, he had to fight the Scots.

Charles I's son, now Charles II, landed in Scotland and was joined by many people. Finally, the Scots invaded England and Cromwell was able to beat the Royalists in a last battle at Worcester on 3 September 1651. He called it a 'crowning mercy'. Charles himself managed to escape. Disguised as a servant, he was smuggled from one loyal house to another until, after many adventures, he reached the south coast. He sailed away from Shoreham in Sussex only just in time: that very day soldiers arrived in Brighton looking for a tall dark man 'above two yards high'.

Cromwell was now fifty-two, a farmer turned soldier, who had never been defeated in battle and was the hero of the new Commonwealth. He was given lands worth £4,000 a year and Hampton Court for his home. Yet he showed no pride in all this. Someone said about him that 'there cannot be *discerned* in him any ambition save for the public good, to which he brings all his spirit and power'.

Cromwell now wanted the Rump to resign so that a new Parliament could be elected. But one day in April 1653 he was told that the Rump was going to pass a bill saying that all the M.P.s there should remain members and choose the other new members. With a group of soldiers Cromwell hurried down to the House of Commons. For a while he listened to the debate until he could bear it no longer. 'I will put an end to your *prating*,' he stood up to cry. 'You are no Parliament. I say you are no Parliament: I will put an end to your sitting. Call them in, call them in.' His soldiers then came in to chase the M.P.s from the House and pull the Speaker from the chair. Then Cromwell noticed the *mace* which always lies in front of the Speaker as a sign of authority. 'What are we to do with this *bauble*?' he cried, 'Take it away!' Cromwell believed he had been driven to do this. He said: 'It's you that have forced me to this.' Later he said that the Rump had become so unpopular that not a dog barked when he ended it.

After this, various experiments in government were tried. In 1653 it was decided that England should be governed by a Lord Protector of the Commonwealth and Parliament. So Oliver Cromwell became His Highness the Lord Protector. He was dressed in ordinary clothes for the ceremony, but everyone knew that he was Protector because of the Army. For the next five years Cromwell did his best to rule well, not so much because he wanted power as because he was the only man who could rule.

But he had to be harsh. Because of plots against the government, anyone suspected was arrested and fined. Ralph Verney, home at last from exile in France, was one of these. He said that 'the soldiers that took me at Claydon on Wednesday last used me very civilly, yet they took all the pistols and swords in the house'. Friends wrote to the government for him, to say that he was no Royalist: 'He was sitting in the Parliament house when his father was killed at Edgehill and sent in voluntarily two horses into the Parliament's army.' After months in prison, Ralph was released, but he still had to pay heavy fines. He wrote at Christmas that year: 'Claydon loves not Christmas: we are all Roundheads on that point to save charges.' (He meant that although the Puritans tried to stop people from making merry at Christmas because they thought it was wrong, he was not keeping Christmas at Claydon because he could not afford it.)

Many people criticized Cromwell, and Colonel Hutchinson was one of these. He would not take any government post under the Protector. When, however, he overheard some men plotting to kill Cromwell, he warned the Lord Protector. Cromwell thanked him and said: 'But, dear Colonel, why will you not come and sit among us?' John

Hutchinson told him plainly that he did not like his ways and thought he was becoming a tyrant like the king.

On 3 September 1658, Oliver Cromwell died without having solved his great problems. He named his eldest son, Richard, to succeed him as Lord Protector, but, as Lucy Hutchinson wrote, 'he was a quiet man, but had not a spirit to succeed his father to manage such a perplexed government'. After eight months he resigned rather than make further trouble, so he is known as 'Tumbledown Dick'. Then there was a time of confusion while different leaders struggled for power. Soon men grew tired of this and began to talk of bringing back the King. General Monk, who had begun as a Royalist and then fought for Parliament, marched his regiment into London in March 1660. He promised to see that a free Parliament was called to decide about the future. First, all the M.P.s who had been elected to the Long Parliament in 1640 were summoned back. Ralph Verney was one of those who returned to take his seat again after such a long time. This was the last of the Long Parliament: they voted that it should end and that there should be elections for a new Parliament. Everyone knew that the new Parliament would invite the King back again.

II

The King Returns

On 25 May 1660, King Charles II landed back in England to be welcomed everywhere on his way from Dover to London. Yet he came back to a very different throne from the one his father had held for most of his years as King. Charles II was restored to the throne as it had been on the day war had been declared on 22 August 1642. This meant that he had to accept all the Acts of the Long Parliament which had been passed between 1640 and 1642. Never again would a King be able to have his own courts, as Charles I had done until they had been abolished by the Long Parliament, or be able to rule as he wished without the consent of Parliament, as Charles I had tried to do.

The Civil War and the period of government by Cromwell had taught us a great deal about the way to govern this country, and what not to do. That is why we still have a Queen ruling through Parliament today. For us, living in Britain now, it is still important that Cavaliers fought Roundheads.

HOW DO WE KNOW?

We know a great deal about the people of the day because they wrote so much about the Civil War. Edward Hyde, who later became Lord Clarendon, thought that the Civil War was a rebellion against the King, and he wrote a book called *The History of the Rebellion*. Many letters of the time have survived, as the Verneys' letters have. Just as Mrs Hutchinson wrote the life of her husband, so Lady Ann Fanshaw wrote about her husband who fought for the King so that her children should know about their father. Although many of the people who fought in the war or wrote about it were people of importance, yet we know something of more ordinary people, too. Nathaniel Wharton, for example, was a London apprentice who fought for Parliament and wrote letters to his master about it.

The first newspapers started in the Civil War. As long as they could, James I and Charles I prevented any printer from publishing news or comments on the government. But when war broke out there was a great demand for news as people wanted to know what was happening, and neither King nor Parliament could stop the printing of news any longer. So thousands of pamphlets were published in these years, giving news of battles or skirmishes, and commenting on what was happening. The pamphlets were small, usually about the size of two or four pages of this book, but they met people's need for news. Some of them began to appear regularly, perhaps once or twice a week, with the same title each time, and so they can be counted as the first newspapers in this country. They had titles like *Diurnall Occurrences* or the *Kingdomes Weekly Intelligencer* or the *London Post*. The King's newspaper which was published in Oxford was called *Mercurius Aulicus* while the one which gave mainly Scottish news was called the *Scottish Dove*. The *London Post* and the *Scottish Dove* began to use woodcuts as illustrations, and so these were the beginnings of the pictures in our newspapers today; they often give us useful illustrations of the castle or town which was the subject of that particular week's news. It is amusing to notice, in reading these early newspapers, how much they anticipated our modern newspapers. Some were very serious and attempted to give accurate news, while others always tried to have something exciting in them, whether it was true or not, to help to sell their newspapers. The serious ones would begin 'It is reported that . . .' while the others would always make sweeping claims like 'many were killed on both sides, but the number of their slain did very far exceed ours.'

There were many poets at this time and you can read some of their poems in the *Oxford Book of Seventeenth Century Verse* or the *Oxford Book of English Verse*. Andrew Marvell was an M.P. for Hull, a Puritan and a supporter of Parliament and of Cromwell. His poem 'An Horatian Ode upon Cromwell's Return from Ireland' is in praise of Cromwell and his victories in Ireland, yet he wrote these lines in admiration of Charles I's dignity and courage at his execution:

> He nothing common did or mean
> Upon that memorable scene
> But with his keener eye
> The axe's edge did try
> Nor called the gods with vulgar spite
> To vindicate his helpless right. . . .

The Marquis of Montrose's poem 'My dear and only love' is the love poem of a real Cavalier. He ends one verse:

> He either fears his fate too much
> Or his deserts are small
> That puts it not into the touch
> To win or lose it all.

There are many other poems by men who fought as Cavaliers, like Richard Lovelace's 'Going to the wars' which he ends

> I could not love thee dear so much
> Loved I not honour more.

You will probably know some of Robert Herrick's poems already, such as his 'Cherry Ripe' and 'To Daffodils'. They remind us of the love of flowers and of country things which many men had at this time.

John Milton, one of our greatest poets, lived through this time: he was a Puritan, and he became Latin Secretary to the Commonwealth.

There are many exciting stories which you can read about the Civil War time. Here are a few of them: Sutherland Ross's *Vagabond Treasure* (Hodder and Stoughton): Rosemary Sutcliffe, *Simon* (O.U.P.): D. Scott Daniell, *Hunt Royal* (Puffin). Some novels for grown-ups which you might enjoy are: Margaret Irwin's *Proud Servant* and *The Bride* which tell the story of Montrose, and her *Stranger Prince* which is about Prince Rupert (Chatto and Windus). Perhaps one of the best is Rose

Macaulay's *They Were Defeated*. If you begin to read this and do not like it, then leave it until you are older: do not spoil it for yourself by reading it too soon. Remember that many of these novels have been written with more sympathy for the Cavaliers than for the Roundheads.

Try to write some scenes for acting, or for 'radio plays' to speak or to put on to tape if you have a tape recorder in school. Good scenes to attempt would be a debate in the Parliament of 1628, Charles I's attempt to arrest the Five Members in 1642, the trial of Charles I, Cromwell and the end of the Rump Parliament. A book like J. S. Millward: *Portraits and Documents: the Seventeenth Century* (Hutchinson) will give you further details of the people and extracts from their speeches.

Other suggestions of things you might like to do, either on your own or in groups are:

Chapter 2. Imagine that you lived in a house like Claydon in these years. Make a wall picture or a model of your house. Describe your house and the furniture you would have in the different rooms. If you make a model, have some of the rooms with open sides so that you can put in wire figures or mount your drawings of people and furniture to put in the rooms. Books which will help you are: D. Hartley and M. M. Elliott, *Life and Work of the People of England: the Seventeenth Century* (Batsford): M. Harrison and A. A. M. Wells, *Picture Source Book for Social History in the Seventeenth Century* (Allen and Unwin): M. and C. B. H. Quennell, *History of Everyday Things in England*, Vol. 2 (Batsford).

Chapters 1, 6, 7. Choose whether you would have been a pikeman, a musketeer or in the cavalry. Describe what you would have worn if you had joined or been pressed into either army. Draw pictures of the different soldiers and their weapons for a wall chart or class book. Measure out the height of a pike and the range of musket fire to get some ideas of size and distance. Write an account of any battle you might have taken part in. Draw battle plans of the main battles or any in your own district. A. H. Burne and Peter Young, *The Great Civil War* (Eyre and Spottiswood) tells you a great deal about the war. You will probably find it too difficult to read unless you are particularly interested in the war, but it has an index of all the main battles and of the regiments which took part in them, so it is in this book that you are most likely to find out what happened in your own district and about the troops which fought there. Another book is Austin Woolrych's *Battles of the English Civil War* (Batsford). Two good books written for boys and girls are R. R. Sellman,

Civil War and Commonwealth (Methuen) and Sutherland Ross, *English Civil War* (Faber). There is also a film for schools: *Civil War in England* (Gaumont British): Part I centres on Edgehill and Part II on Marston Moor.

Chapters 3 and 7. Describe what you would have worn had you lived at that time. Make a class book of the clothes worn by you and your family. Dress wire or cardboard figures to go with a model of a house, or paste your pictures on to a wall picture. These books will help you: Iris Brook, *English Costume in the Seventeenth Century* (Black); C. W. and P. Cunnington, *Handbook of Costume in the Seventeenth Century* (Faber).

Chapters 4 and 5. Imagine that, like Sir Edmund Verney, you are an M.P. in the 1628 Parliament and in the two Parliaments of 1640. Write letters home to your family to tell them what is happening. You can show which side you are on by the way you word your letters.

Chapter 6. Write a letter to a friend after August 1642 to say what you have decided to do and why. Imagine that your friend disagrees with you: perhaps is going to join the other side or is not going to fight at all if he can help it. Write a scene in which you discuss this with one another.

Chapter 9. Imagine that you managed to get into Westminster Hall to watch the King's trial, and describe what happens. J. D. Muddiman, H. Ross Williamson and C. V. Wedgwood have all written books on the trial of the King: you may be able to get one of them from your public library if you need more detail.

Chapter 10. Write an account of Cromwell's life, describing what you think of him, showing whether you are one of his admirers or not. There is a good life of Cromwell written for young people, N. Martin: *Our Chief of Men* (Longmans) and you could probably read Peter Young's *Oliver Cromwell* (Batsford), too. There is a record of the speeches of Oliver Cromwell (H.M.V. in the Laureate series).

Finding out about the Civil War in your own town or district.

Go to your public library to see if the librarians can help you. You may find books with pictures or maps or battle plans which you will want, and you can use the index to find out about a particular place without reading the whole book. For example, if you live in Sussex, Thomas Stanford, *Sussex in the Great Civil War* is too long and difficult to read right through but you would enjoy the chapter on the young King Charles II's escape after the battle of Worcester in 1651: this would give you a wonderful story to turn into a play. You may be lucky, and find that your library has a collection of the pamphlets and newspapers printed at the time. If, for example, you live in Newcastle upon Tyne, most of the pamphlets and letters which tell the story of the long siege of Newcastle during the Civil War are in the British Museum in London or in the University Library and you could not see those, but there are some in the Central Reference Library in Newcastle and your teacher might arrange with the Librarian to let you see them. This is true of many town and county public libraries.

Your public library will also have a copy of *Historic Castles, Houses and Gardens open to the Public*. See if you have any places of interest for this period, either in your own district or while you are on holiday. In Buckinghamshire, for example, you can visit Claydon House. The part of the house which is open to the public has been built since the seventeenth century: you cannot visit the part in which Sir Edmund Verney and his family lived because the Verney family still live in it today. But you can see that part of the house from the outside and visit the little church nearby with its monuments to Sir Edmund and Ralph.

In London, you can visit the Banqueting Hall in Whitehall, see Westminster Hall where the trial of Charles I took place, see the statue of Oliver Cromwell outside the Houses of Parliament, and the statue of Charles I looking down Whitehall where the crowds once stood to watch his execution. There is a good collection of the armour and weapons of the period in the Tower of London, of costume in the Victoria and Albert Museum, and in the London Museum in Kensington Palace you can see one of the two shirts which Charles I wore on the day he was executed – and you can still see the bloodstains on it.

We cannot all be as lucky as the children who go to school near Newbury in a house which was a stronghold for the King, and where they can see, in one of the classrooms, the bullet marks in the panelling where Charles I narrowly escaped being shot as he stood near the window before the second battle of Newbury. Wherever you live, however, you will almost certainly be able to visit some castle or house or museum where you can see something of the homes of the people of this period, and of their costumes, furniture and weapons, which will help to bring the years of the Civil War near to you.

GLOSSARY

arbitrator : one who judges in a dispute

bandolier : leather band with containers for ammunition

bauble : toy

Bill of Attainder : Act of Parliament to declare someone a traitor

breach : break

cock : lever in gunlock raised ready for release by trigger

covenant : solemn promise

to discern : to see

doublet : man's short coat

eloquence : fine speaking

to encroach : to take what does not belong to you

farthingale : wide, stiffened skirt

frailty : weakness

fundamental : something which is a foundation

groat : small coin like a penny

hereditary : possession passed on by right from father to son

implacable : never-ending in hatred

imposition : heavy burden

impregnable : not possible to capture

lamentable : something causing sorrow

mace : ornamented stick carried in front of an official to mark authority.

monopoly : see *patent*

musketeer : soldier carrying a musket (gun)

to pacify : to calm an angry person

patent : right given to one person only to make, sell or do something

pertaining to : belonging to

pewter : mixture of lead and tin used to make dishes, mugs etc.

pikeman : soldier carrying a long pike (spear)

posterity : children, children's children and so on

pottage : soup or stew

prating : talking

pressed man : man forced into the army

primer : powder used to spark off the charge of gunpowder

remonstrance : strong complaint

stature : a person's height

tasset : armour to guard legs

unbiased : fair-minded

vestment : robe, especially that worn by clergymen for Church services

to wrest : to snatch